COMMITTED TO MEMORY

Edited, with an Introduction, by

JOHN HOLLANDER

❧❀❧

❧❀❧

RIVERHEAD BOOKS
NEW YORK

COMMITTED
TO MEMORY

100 BEST POEMS

TO MEMORIZE

Most Riverhead Books are available at special quantity discounts for bulk purchases for sales promotions, premiums, fund-raising, or educational use. Special books, or book excerpts, can also be created to fit specific needs.

For details, write: Special Markets, The Berkley Publishing Group, 200 Madison Avenue, New York, New York 10016.

Riverhead Books
Published by The Berkley Publishing Group
A member of Penguin Putnam Inc.
200 Madison Avenue
New York, New York 10016

The publishers would like to thank the authors, publishers, and literary representatives listed on pages 195 and 196 for permission to reprint from copyrighted and previously published material.

Copyright © 1996 by The Academy of American Poets
Introduction copyright © 1996 by John Hollander
Book design by Cynthia Krupat
Cover design by James R. Harris

Books & Co./Turtle Point edition published in 1996.
Books & Co./Turtle Point ISBN: 1-885983-15-8
First Riverhead trade paperback edition: November 1997

The Putnam Berkley World Wide Web site address is
http://www.berkley.com

The Library of Congress Cataloging-in-Publication Data

Committed to memory: 100 best poems to memorize / edited, with an introduction by John Hollander ; advisory committee,
Eavan Boland . . . [et al.].—1st Riverhead trade pbk. ed.
        p. cm.
    ISBN 1-57322-646-7
    1. English poetry. 2. American Poetry. I. Hollander, John.
II. Boland, Eavan.
PR1175.C6425   1997
821.008—dc21   97-10450
                                          CIP

PRINTED IN THE UNITED STATES OF AMERICA

10   9   8   7   6   5   4   3   2

CONTENTS

SONGS

MEDITATIONS

INTRODUCTION

In Plato's *Phaedrus*, Socrates tells a story about the invention of writing, in which the Egyptian god Thoth shows his written characters to another god, Ammon, who rebukes him: "This discovery of yours will create forgetfulness in the learners' souls, because they will not use their memories; they will trust to the external written characters and not remember themselves." There were stories and songs—and songs that told stories—long before there was any writing, and they were kept alive not in libraries but through a cycle of reciting, listening, memorizing, and reciting anew. Each language drew on its own resources of sound structure for the aural patterns—the kinds of rhythm and repetition of sounds, words, phrases, and kinds of phrase—that made spoken poetry sound very different from ordinary discourse and, in particular, easier to commit to memory. But even after almost three millennia of written literature, poetry retains its appeal to the ear as well as to the eye; to hear a poem read aloud by someone who understands it, and who wishes to share that understanding with someone else, can be a crucial experience, instructing the silently reading eye ever thereafter to hear what it is seeing. Better yet is reading aloud that way oneself.

This is a gathering of a hundred-and-some poems chosen specifically for memorization, and for the particularly intense kind of silent reading with which a reader prepares to remember them. Even fifty years ago—let alone a hundred—this collection might have seemed an anomaly, in that most readers tended to commit to memory short poems, or passages from longer ones, that had particularly affected them. Moreover, they had been trained at school to memorize, and to recite from memory, a considerable number of specimens of verse in English, ranging from major poetry to relics of nineteenth-century recitation pieces. It is easier to memorize texts when you are younger than when older; but the practice, learned early, can be maintained. And thus, for matured readers, memorizing a poem or passage you liked, rather than one which had been required of you (but which, of course, you may very well have gotten to like eventually), was almost a matter of course. But this is no longer the case, and memorization—along with training in reading prose aloud, of which another word shortly—has disappeared from most school curricula.

At the same time, we have suffered a rapidly accelerating decay in the quality of oral performance of text in public life: television and radio newscasters fumble pronunciations and read even minimal prose with a decreasing sense of how the written word makes sense when sounded aloud. Persons appointed by commercial or governmental institutions to speak for them frequently read text aloud as if they don't understand even the grammar of what they are mouthing. Now, as we anxiously reassess the condition of education in our country, the relations among reading, listening, and understanding become more significant. Nowhere are these relations more intensely embodied than in the matter of spoken verse. And nowhere does one learn better how to read either verse or prose aloud than by recitation from memory. Needless to say, it is an element of true literacy to be able to recognize in fiction, essay, and later poetry (with a sense of familiarity rather than by consulting a professorial footnote) the allusions to passages of great poetry of the past—not merely to Shakespeare and the King James Version of the Bible—that fill the stream of discourse.

THIS SELECTION

The selection of poems for this collection was a collaborative effort between the editor and the Advisory Committee. All had memorized poetry when young and have since developed various kinds of poetic sensibilities of their own. Yet this is not merely a collection of favorite shorter poetry, but one carefully chosen for the pleasure and profit with which the poems would reward memorization and recital by younger readers.

A number of questions guided the choosing here. For one thing, the free verse of modernist and later poetry is very much harder to memorize than the accentual verse of nursery rhyme and older popular song, or the accentual-syllabic verse—so-called iambic, trochaic, dactylic and so forth—of literary poetry in English from Chaucer on. Rhyming accentual-syllabic verse is always a great aid to memorizing. It will be noticed that all but a few of the selections here exhibit this kind of design.

Length is, of course, a criterion as well: a single couplet would be too short (even a great epigram like John Donne's imaginary epitaph for Hero and Leander: "Both robbed of air, we both lie in one ground, / Both whom one fire had burnt, one water drowned," with its invocation of the four elements and its interplay of "both" and "one"). An otherwise wonderful set-piece like Gray's "Elegy Written in a Country Churchyard," at 128 lines, would be too long (although celebrated individual quatrains from it might be taken as short pieces in themselves—one thinks, for example, of "The boast of heraldry, the pomp of pow'r, / And all that beauty, all that wealth e'er gave, / Awaits alike th' inevitable hour, / The paths of glory lead but to the grave."). The poems included here range in length from the extreme instance of Walter Savage Landor's wonderful quatrain "On His Seventy-fifth Birthday" to Tennyson's "Ulysses," with seventy-three lines. And they range in degree of familiarity from Coleridge's "Kubla Khan" and Poe's "To Helen" and Dickinson's "Because I could not stop for Death" to Edwin Muir's "The Animals" and Trumbull Stickney's "Mnemosyne," poems of which most readers will not have heard.

Otherwise, these poems embrace a wide variety of genres, structures, forms, patterns, and schemes. The grouping indicated in the Contents reflects this variety in that classifications range from the formal to the thematic and rhetorical, from the sonnet (which has remained a remarkably productive loom on which remarkably different fabrics have been woven in English for over four and a half centuries) through the explicitly narrative (whether an older ballad or, like those of E. A. Robinson and D. G. Rossetti in this collection, more akin to the modern short story). The genre called "lyrical poetry" has come to include so much during the literary history of the past four hundred years that its boundaries are hard to trace: most of the poems of modernity could be called "lyric." Some of them will indeed be song-texts without the music; some will be pseudo-song-texts that have so thoroughly incorporated and internalized the figurative music of their own patterns of sound and sense that setting them to music would seem cacophonous—the French poet Paul Valéry compared it to looking at a fine painting in the light coming through a stained-glass window. But the reader and rememberer will feel throughout this section the point of the title that Yeats gave to a group of lyrics in one of his later books: "Words for Music Perhaps."

3

We speak of memorizing as getting something "by heart," which really means "by head." But getting a poem or prose passage truly "by heart" implies getting it by mind and memory and understanding and delight. There are many ways to memorize texts of any kind, but for verse, reading lines aloud and listening to yourself as you recite them is crucial. It is partly like memorizing a song whose tune is that of the words themselves. The kind of ordering or sequence or logical progression of parts of the poem—lines, groups of lines, stanzas, sections, verse paragraphs—will figure strongly in the way we hold it together in memory.

Different poems get remembered in different ways—a ballad or other narrative poem as opposed to a lyrical poem that unfolds in its own kind of sequence—a strophic poem or a passage of rhymed or blank verse that moves on more discursively. In memorizing and reciting, one becomes even more deeply aware of pattern and structure: stanza forms, repeating patterns of anaphora (as in Thomas Carew's lovely "Ask me no more") or refrain.[*] We notice, too, how the argument or catalogue or narrative unfolds itself through the stanzas, sections, or even groups of lines.

Certainly a poem's structure—the way in which it's put together—becomes very important; as you memorize a sonnet, you almost get to feel the way in which it can be argumentative or more expressively meditative in its structure. Shakespeare's sonnet #18: "Shall I compare thee to a summer's day? / Thou art more lovely and more temperate," for example, is arranged in quatrains and a summary couplet, and yet its pattern is that of a catalogue of comparisons followed, in the last six lines, by a set of transcending contrasts. It avoids the logical unfolding of "If . . . And . . . Then . . . Yes" so frequent in that mode. Compare it with the arrangement in the sonnet of the catalogue of beautiful sights in Wordsworth's "Composed upon Westminster Bridge." On the other hand, memorizing will make clearer than even the most studious written analysis the difference in the ways in which the octave-sestet pattern in the "Italian form" of the sonnet[†] can be de-

---

[*]For explanations and examples of technical terms, see John Hollander, *Rhyme's Reason* (New Haven, 1989). For "anaphora" and "refrain," see p. 78 and pp. 37–46, respectively.
[†]Ibid., pp. 19–21.

4

ployed: John Donne's "At the round earth's imagin'd corners" expands one long complex imperative in its first eight lines; then, starting with a "But . . .," qualifies the octave in the final six lines of the sestet. But Milton's famous sonnet on his blindness systematically bridges what we might think of as a logical space of retraction or qualification usually found between octave and sestet. His sentence "But patience, to prevent / That murmur, soon replies . . ." connects the lines and even the sections that are almost like two stanzas in this sort of sonnet, with a strong enjambment.*

When memorizing a poem, too, we become aware of the resonances of particular words. For example, a memorized reading of Shelley's "Ozymandias" might very well come up with the two meanings of "mock" in "The hand that mocked them"—*imitate* (here, in sculpture) and *ridicule or deride*. And note the change of the mood of the single auxiliary verb "do" in the first refrain of Dylan Thomas's "Do not go gentle . . ." from imperative to indicative in the central tercets, or the subtle shifts in meaning of the second refrain. This poem also exemplifies the form called "villanelle."† With its repeating double refrains, a poem like this is rather easy to memorize; on the other hand, reciting it aloud, *performing* it—as will be seen in a moment—presents interesting challenges to the intonation and emphasis given to repeated elements.

PERFORMANCE

Having recorded a poem in your memory is one thing. Playing what's been recorded is another. A perfectly played and recorded tape or CD can sound like a disaster on faulty equipment handled ineptly. So with a memorized text. Performing a poem can mean any one of a number of things. Anyone who has heard a poetry reading cannot fail to observe that some poets read their work aloud very well indeed. They read the poems for their meaning, rather than to express their personal presences: the "performance" in this case is more like that of a musician playing—and thereby interpreting—a solo piano piece, say, than it is like what has gotten to be called "performance art" (a sword-swallower or fire-eater or stand-up comic).

*Ibid., p. 15.
†Ibid., pp. 40, 83.

In reciting a poem aloud, you are not like an actor, coming to understand, and then to feel yourself in a dramatic part, a fictional person. It's rather that you come to understand, and then to be, the voice of the poem itself.

Several matters are crucial to a good playback of what your memory has stored. One of the first is that of voice itself. I've noticed that college and even graduate students today, when asked to read aloud in class, mutter and mumble rather than speaking out—or speaking up. Doubtless, some of this can be attributed to a fear of sounding pompous, orotund, empty and phony, qualities associated with the loud and elaborated speechifying of dubious politicians and preachers, or of simply shouting like the voice-overs on automobile commercials. But whatever its general or particular personal causes, this reticence has to be overcome, and a little practice will allow you to project your voice, finding the right level without seeming over-loud or shrill. Then comes intonation, the matter of the sound of making sense. It is through control of tone of voice—of pitch and stress—that we orally represent the various ways in which short sentences or clauses, and long, periodic ones, perhaps stretching across many lines, can be understood. Contrastive stress is very important in English—consider the difference between "*this* book, *that* book" and "this *book*, that *cup*," and the way the italicization indicates which of the two syllables in each pair would be stressed. Poems are full of invisibly italicized contrasts of this kind, and your reading should realize these.

Central also to reading verse aloud is the handling of enjambment. Obvious cases are those of, say, the lines from Milton's sonnet "On His Blindness" quoted earlier. Or these from Keats's "To Autumn": "And sometimes like a gleaner thou dost keep / Steady thy laden head across a brook"—where you would want to override the line-break almost completely in your reading of it, instead of pausing as you might naturally do at the rhyme-word, "keep." But many enjambments are gentler and subtler than these, the line-break cutting into the syntax less violently, and you eventually learn to deal with these, only gently acknowledging by your tone and near-pause the interplay of line-end and sentence-flow at each point.

Tone is particularly important in comical or light verse: too much underlining of what the lines themselves are clearly doing is like jabbing a finger in the shoulder of a listener as you tell a joke to make him or her "get the point." Less obvious but even more important can be the emotional and rhetorical "tone" of a dramatic

6

lyric, like Blake's "The Tyger," or a monologue, like Browning's "My Last Duchess"—in each case you have to decide who the speakers are, what they know or realize about what they're saying, and so forth. The more you understand a poem and see its complexities and depths, the more you will be able to do when reading it aloud.

As you recite a poem, you know how long it is, and how long each section or part of it is. Your listeners—unable as silent readers do to glance down the page or riffle through successive ones—may not. As in a musical performance, your reading, as well as acknowledging the section-breaks, will have to build toward its conclusion. And while a melodramatic, grandiose, or corny ending is always unfortunate, it is still necessary to indicate with your voice in some way that the poem has come to an end. If the poem ends wittily or pointedly, tying up its formal or narrative or conceptual loose ends in any way, you need do little to color this with your tone. If it fades away, as many lyrics do, you may have to do a bit more.

Hearing enough good recitation will enable you not only to memorize, but also to read other poetry with its sound in your mental ear. Of later twentieth-century poets, Richard Wilbur, the late James Merrill, Anthony Hecht, W. S. Merwin, and Thom Gunn are all outstanding public readers of poetry, and any recordings of their readings will be valuable guides to the questions just discussed. And finally, in the case of any good poem, remember the old proverb about thrift and the revision of it by the Duchess in *Alice in Wonderland*: "Take care of the sense and the sounds will take care of themselves."

JOHN HOLLANDER

SONNETS

ELIZABETH BISHOP

[1911–1979]

Sonnet

I am in need of music that would flow
Over my fretful, feeling finger-tips,
Over my bitter-tainted, trembling lips,
With melody, deep, clear, and liquid-slow.
Oh, for the healing swaying, old and low,
Of some song sung to rest the tired dead,
A song to fall like water on my head,
And over quivering limbs, dream flushed to glow!

There is a magic made by melody:
A spell of rest, and quiet breath, and cool
Heart, that sinks through fading colors deep
To the subaqueous stillness of the sea,
And floats forever in a moon-green pool,
Held in the arms of rhythm and of sleep.

JOHN DONNE
[1572–1631]

At the round earths imagin'd corners

At the round earths imagin'd corners, blow
Your trumpets, Angells, and arise, arise
From death, you numberlesse infinities
Of soules, and to your scattred bodies goe,
All whom the flood did, and fire shall o'erthrow,
All whom warre, dearth, age, agues, tyrannies,
Despaire, law, chance, hath slaine, and you whose eyes,
Shall behold God, and never tast deaths woe.
But let them sleepe, Lord, and mee mourne a space,
For, if above all these, my sinnes abound,
'Tis late to aske abundance of thy grace,
When wee are there; here on this lowly ground,
Teach mee how to repent; for that's as good
As if thou'hadst seal'd my pardon, with thy blood.

JOHN KEATS
[1795–1821]

On First Looking into Chapman's Homer

Much have I traveled in the realms of gold
   And many goodly states and kingdoms seen;
   Round many western islands have I been
Which bards in fealty to Apollo hold.
Oft of one wide expanse had I been told
   That deep-browed Homer ruled as his demesne;
   Yet never did I breathe its pure serene
Till I heard Chapman speak out loud and bold:
Then felt I like some watcher of the skies
   When a new planet swims into his ken;
Or like stout Cortez when with eagle eyes
   He stared at the Pacific—and all his men
Looked at each other with a wild surmise—
   Silent, upon a peak in Darien.

EMMA LAZARUS

[1849 – 1887]

The New Colossus

Not like the brazen giant of Greek fame,
With conquering limbs astride from land to land;
Here at our sea-washed, sunset gates shall stand
A mighty woman with a torch, whose flame
Is the imprisoned lightning, and her name
Mother of Exiles. From her beacon-hand
Glows world-wide welcome; her mild eyes command
The air-bridged harbor that twin cities frame.
"Keep, ancient lands, your storied pomp!" cries she
With silent lips. "Give me your tired, your poor,
Your huddled masses yearning to breathe free,
The wretched refuse of your teeming shore.
Send these, the homeless, tempest-tost to me,
I lift my lamp beside the golden door!"

GEORGE MEREDITH

[1828–1909]

Lucifer in Starlight

On a starred night Prince Lucifer uprose.
Tired of his dark dominion swung the fiend
Above the rolling ball in cloud part screened,
Where sinners hugged their specter of repose.
Poor prey to his hot fit of pride were those.
And now upon his western wing he leaned,
Now his huge bulk o'er Afric's sands careened,
Now the black planet shadowed Arctic snows.
Soaring through wider zones that pricked his scars
With memory of the old revolt from Awe,
He reached a middle height, and at the stars,
Which are the brain of heaven, he looked, and sank.
Around the ancient track marched, rank on rank,
The army of unalterable law.

JOHN MILTON
[1608–1674]

On His Blindness

When I consider how my light is spent,
  Ere half my days, in this dark world and wide,
  And that one Talent which is death to hide,
  Lodg'd with me useless, though my Soul more bent
To serve therewith my Maker, and present
  My true account, least he returning chide,
  Doth God exact day-labour, light deny'd,
  I fondly ask; But patience to prevent
That murmur, soon replies, God doth not need
  Either man's work or his own gifts, who best
  Bear his milde yoak, they serve him best, his State
Is Kingly. Thousands at his bidding speed
  And post o're Land and Ocean without rest:
  They also serve who only stand and waite.

JOHN CROWE RANSOM
[1888–1974]

Piazza Piece

—I am a gentleman in a dust coat trying
To make you hear. Your ears are soft and small
And listen to an old man not at all,
They want the young men's whispering and sighing.
But see the roses on your trellis dying
And hear the spectral singing of the moon;
For I must have my lovely lady soon,
I am a gentleman in a dust coat trying.

—I am a lady young in beauty waiting
Until my truelove comes, and then we kiss.
But what gray man among the vines is this
Whose words are dry and faint as in a dream?
Back from my trellis, sir, before I scream!
I am a lady young in beauty waiting.

WILLIAM SHAKESPEARE

[1564–1616]

Sonnet #18

Shall I compare thee to a summer's day?
Thou art more lovely and more temperate.
Rough winds do shake the darling buds of May,
And summer's lease hath all too short a date.
Sometime too hot the eye of heaven shines,
And often is his gold complexion dimmed;
And every fair from fair sometime declines,
By chance, or nature's changing course, untrimmed;
But thy eternal summer shall not fade,
Nor lose possession of that fair thou ow'st,
Nor shall Death brag thou wand'rest in his shade,
When in eternal lines to time thou grow'st.
  So long as men can breathe or eyes can see,
  So long lives this, and this gives life to thee.

WILLIAM SHAKESPEARE

[1 5 6 4 – 1 6 1 6]

Sonnet #55

Not marble nor the gilded monuments
Of princes shall outlive this powerful rhyme;
But you shall shine more bright in these contents
Than unswept stone, besmear'd with sluttish time.
When wasteful war shall statues overturn,
And broils root out the work of masonry,
Nor Mars his sword nor war's quick fire shall burn
The living record of your memory.
'Gainst death and all-oblivious enmity
Shall you pace forth; your praise shall still find room,
Even in the eyes of all posterity
That wear this world out to the ending doom.
  So, till the judgment that yourself arise,
    You live in this, and dwell in lovers' eyes.

PERCY BYSSHE SHELLEY

[1792–1822]

Ozymandias

I met a traveler from an antique land
Who said: Two vast and trunkless legs of stone
Stand in the desert . . . Near them, on the sand,
Half sunk, a shattered visage lies, whose frown,
And wrinkled lip, and sneer of cold command,
Tell that its sculptor well those passions read
Which yet survive, stamped on these lifeless things,
The hand that mocked them, and the heart that fed:
And on the pedestal these words appear:
"My name is Ozymandias, king of kings:
Look on my works, ye Mighty, and despair!"
Nothing beside remains. Round the decay
Of that colossal wreck, boundless and bare
The lone and level sands stretch far away.

WILLIAM WORDSWORTH
[1770–1850]

Composed upon Westminster Bridge
Sept. 3, 1802

Earth has not anything to show more fair:
* Dull would he be of soul who could pass by
A sight so touching in its majesty:
This City now doth, like a garment, wear
The beauty of the morning; silent, bare,
Ships, towers, domes, theatres, and temples lie
Open unto the fields, and to the sky;
All bright and glittering in the smokeless air.
Never did sun more beautifully steep
In his first splendour, valley, rock, or hill;
Ne'er saw I, never felt, a calm so deep!
The river glideth at his own sweet will:
Dear God! the very houses seem asleep;
And all that mighty heart is lying still!

And all that mighty heart is lying still!

SONGS

JOSEPH ADDISON

[1672–1719]

The Spacious Firmament on high

The Spacious Firmament on high,
With all the blue Ethereal Sky,
And spangled Heav'ns, a Shining Frame,
Their great Original proclaim:
Th' unwearied Sun, from day to day,
Does his Creator's Pow'r display,
And publishes to every Land
The Work of an Almighty Hand.

Soon as the Evening Shades prevail,
The Moon takes up the wondrous Tale,
And nightly to the list'ning Earth
Repeats the Story of her Birth:
Whilst all the Stars that round her burn,
And all the Planets, in their turn,
Confirm the Tidings as they rowl,
And spread the Truth from Pole to Pole.

What though, in solemn Silence, all
Move round the dark terrestrial Ball?
What tho' nor real Voice nor Sound
Amid their radiant Orbs be found?

In Reason's Ear they all rejoice,
And utter forth a glorious Voice,
For ever singing, as they shine,
The Hand that made us is Divine.

W. H. AUDEN

[1907–1973]

Lay your sleeping head, my love

Lay your sleeping head, my love,
Human on my faithless arm;
Time and fevers burn away
Individual beauty from
Thoughtful children, and the grave
Proves the child ephemeral:
But in my arms till break of day
Let the living creature lie,
Mortal, guilty, but to me
The entirely beautiful.

Soul and body have no bounds:
To lovers as they lie upon
Her tolerant enchanted slope
In their ordinary swoon,
Grave the vision Venus sends
Of supernatural sympathy,
Universal love and hope;

While an abstract insight wakes
Among the glaciers and the rocks
The hermit's sensual ecstasy.

Certainty, fidelity
On the stroke of midnight pass
Like vibrations of a bell,
And fashionable madmen raise
Their pedantic boring cry:
Every farthing of the cost,
All the dreaded cards foretell,
Shall be paid, but from this night
Not a whisper, not a thought,
Not a kiss nor look be lost.

Beauty, midnight, vision dies:
Let the winds of dawn that blow
Softly round your dreaming head
Such a day of sweetness show
Eye and knocking heart may bless,
Find the mortal world enough;
Noons of dryness see you fed
By the involuntary powers,
Nights of insult let you pass
Watched by every human love.

WILLIAM BLAKE

[1757–1827]

FROM *Milton: And did those feet*

And did those feet in ancient time
Walk upon England's mountains green?
And was the holy Lamb of God
On England's pleasant pastures seen?

And did the Countenance Divine
Shine forth upon our clouded hills?
And was Jerusalem builded here,
Among these dark Satanic Mills?

Bring me my Bow of burning gold:
Bring me my Arrows of desire:
Bring me my Spear: O clouds unfold!
Bring me my Chariot of fire!

I will not cease from Mental Fight,
Nor shall my Sword sleep in my hand,
Till we have built Jerusalem
In England's green & pleasant Land.

WILLIAM BLAKE

[1757–1827]

The Tyger

Tyger! Tyger! burning bright
In the forests of the night,
What immortal hand or eye
Could frame thy fearful symmetry?

In what distant deeps or skies
Burnt the fire of thine eyes?
On what wings dare he aspire?
What the hand, dare seize the fire?

And what shoulder, & what art,
Could twist the sinews of thy heart?
And when thy heart began to beat,
What dread hand? & what dread feet?

What the hammer? what the chain?
In what furnace was thy brain?
What the anvil? what dread grasp
Dare its deadly terrors clasp?

When the stars threw down their spears,
And water'd heaven with their tears,
Did he smile his work to see?
Did he who made the Lamb make thee?

Tyger! Tyger! burning bright
In the forests of the night,
What immortal hand or eye
Dare frame thy fearful symmetry?

ROBERT BURNS

[1759–1796]

Afton Water

Flow gently, sweet Afton, among thy green braes,
Flow gently, I'll sing thee a song in thy praise;
My Mary's asleep by thy murmuring stream,
Flow gently, sweet Afton, disturb not her dream.

Thou stock-dove whose echo resounds through the glen,
Ye wild whistling blackbirds in yon thorny den,
Thou green-crested lapwing, thy screaming forbear,
I charge you disturb not my slumbering fair.

How lofty, sweet Afton, thy neighboring hills,
Far marked with the courses of clear winding rills;
There daily I wander as noon rises high,
My flocks and my Mary's sweet cot in my eye.

How pleasant thy banks and green valleys below,
Where wild in the woodlands the primroses blow;
There oft as mild evening weeps over the lea,
The sweet-scented birk shades my Mary and me.

Thy crystal stream, Afton, how lovely it glides,
And winds by the cot where my Mary resides;
How wanton thy waters her snowy feet lave,
As gathering sweet flowerets she stems thy clear wave.

Flow gently, sweet Afton, among thy green braes,
Flow gently, sweet river, the theme of my lays;
My Mary's asleep by thy murmuring stream,
Flow gently, sweet Afton, disturb not her dream.

ROBERT BURNS

[1759–1796]

A Red, Red Rose

O my luve's like a red, red rose,
  That's newly sprung in June;
O my luve's like the melodie
  That's sweetly played in tune.

As fair art thou, my bonnie lass,
  So deep in luve am I;
And I will luve thee still, my dear,
Till a' the seas gang dry.

Till a' the seas gang dry, my dear,
  And the rocks melt wi' the sun:
O I will love thee still, my dear,
  While the sands o' life shall run.

And fare thee weel, my only luve,
  And fare thee weel awhile!
And I will come again, my luve,
  Though it were ten thousand mile.

GEORGE G. N., LORD BYRON
[1788–1824]

So we'll go no more a roving

So, we'll go no more a roving
    So late into the night,
Though the heart be still as loving,
    And the moon be still as bright.

For the sword outwears its sheath,
    And the soul wears out the breast,
And the heart must pause to breathe,
    And love itself have rest.

Though the night was made for loving,
    And the day returns too soon,
Yet we'll go no more a roving
    By the light of the moon.

THOMAS CAREW
[C. 1598 – C. 1640]

Ask me no more

Ask me no more where Jove bestows,
When June is past, the fading rose;
For in your beauty's orient deep,
These flowers, as in their causes, sleep.

Ask me no more whither do stray
The golden atoms of the day;
For in pure love heaven did prepare
Those powders to enrich your hair.

Ask me no more whither doth haste
The nightingale when May is past;
For in your sweet dividing throat
She winters, and keeps warm her note.

Ask me no more where those stars light,
That downwards fall in dead of night;
For in your eyes they sit, and there
Fixéd become, as in their sphere.

Ask me no more if east or west
The phoenix builds her spicy nest;
For unto you at last she flies,
And in your fragrant bosom dies.

WALTER DE LA MARE

[1873–1956]

The Song of the Mad Prince

Who said, 'Peacock Pie'?
  The old King to the sparrow:
Who said, 'Crops are ripe'?
  Rust to the harrow:
Who said, 'Where sleeps she now?
  Where rests she now her head,
Bathed in eve's loveliness'?———
  That's what I said.

Who said, 'Ay, mum's the word'?
  Sexton to willow:
Who said, 'Green dusk for dreams,
  Moss for a pillow'?
Who said, 'All Time's delight
  Hath she for narrow bed;
Life's troubled bubble broken'?———
  That's what I said.

EMILY DICKINSON

[1830–1886]

Dear March—Come in—

Dear March—Come in—
How glad I am—
I hoped for you before—
Put down your Hat—
You must have walked—
How out of Breath you are—
Dear March, how are you, and the Rest—
Did you leave Nature well—
Oh March, Come right up stairs with me—
I have so much to tell—

I got your Letter, and the Birds—
The Maples never knew that you were coming—till I called
I declare–how Red their Faces grew—
But March, forgive me—and
All those Hills you left for me to Hue—
There was no Purple suitable—
You took it all with you—

Who knocks? That April.
Lock the Door—
I will not be pursued—
He stayed away a Year to call
When I am occupied—
But trifles look so trivial
As soon as you have come

That Blame is just as dear as Praise
And Praise as mere as Blame—

Break of Day

'Tis true, 'tis day; what though it be?
O wilt thou therefore rise from me?
Why should we rise, because 'tis light?
Did we lie down, because 'twas night?
Love, which in spite of darkness brought us hither,
Should in despite of light keep us together.

Light hath no tongue, but is all eye;
If it could speak as well as spy,
This were the worst that it could say,
That being well, I fain would stay,
And that I loved my heart and honor so,
That I would not from him, that had them, go.

Must business thee from hence remove?
O, that's the worst disease of love.
The poor, the foul, the false, love can
Admit, but not the busied man.
He which hath business, and makes love, doth do
Such wrong, as when a married man doth woo.

PAUL LAURENCE DUNBAR

[1872–1906]

When Malindy Sings

G'way an' quit dat noise, Miss Lucy—
  Put dat music book away;
What's de use to keep on tryin'?
  Ef you practise twell you're gray,
You cain't sta't no notes a-flyin'
  Lak de ones dat rants and rings
F'om de kitchen to de big woods
  When Malindy sings.

You ain't got de nachel o'gans
  Fu' to make de soun' come right,
You ain't got de tu'ns an' twistin's
  Fu' to make it sweet an' light.
Tell you one thing now, Miss Lucy,
  An' I'm tellin' you fu' true,
When hit comes to raal right singin',
  'T ain't no easy thing to do.

Easy 'nough fu' folks to hollah,
  Lookin' at de lines an' dots,

When dey ain't no one kin sence it,
    An' de chune comes in, in spots;
But fu' real malojous music,
    Dat jes' strikes yo' hea't and clings,
Jes' you stan' an' listen wif me
    When Malindy sings.

Ain't you nevah hyeahd Malindy?
    Blessed soul, tek up de cross!
Look hyeah, ain't you jokin', honey?
    Well, you don't know whut you los'.
Y' ought to hyeah dat gal a-wa'blin',
    Robins, la'ks, an' all dem things,
Heish dey moufs an' hides dey face.
    When Malindy sings.

Fiddlin' man jes' stop his fiddlin',
    Lay his fiddle on de she'f;
Mockin'-bird quit tryin' to whistle,
    'Cause he jes' so shamed hisse'f.
Folks a-playin' on de banjo
    Draps dey fingahs on de strings—
Bless yo' soul—fu'gits to move em,
    When Malindy sings.

She jes' spreads huh mouf and hollahs,
    "Come to Jesus," twell you hyeah
Sinnahs' tremblin' steps and voices
    Timid-lak a-drawin' neah;
Den she tu'ns to "Rock of Ages,"
    Simply to de cross she clings,
An' you fin' yo' teahs a-drappin'
    When Malindy sings.

Who dat says dat humble praises
   Wif de Master nevah counts?
Heish yo' mouf, I hyeah dat music,
   Ez hit rises up an' mounts—
Floatin' by de hills an' valleys,
   Way above dis buryin' sod,
Ez hit makes its way in glory
   To de very gates of God!

Oh, hit's sweetah dan de music
   Of an edicated band;
An' hit's dearah dan de battle's
   Song o' triumph in de lan'.
It seems holier dan evenin'
   When de solemn chu'ch bell rings,
Ez I sit an' ca'mly listen
   While Malindy sings.

Towsah, stop dat ba'kin', hyeah me!
   Mandy, mek dat chile keep still;
Don't you hyeah de echoes callin'
   F'om de valley to de hill?
Let me listen, I can hyeah it,
   Th'oo de bresh of angels' wings,
Sof' an' sweet, "Swing Low,
   Sweet Chariot,"
Ez Malindy sings.

RALPH WALDO EMERSON
[1803–1882]

Concord Hymn

By the rude bridge that arched the flood,
　Their flag to April's breeze unfurled,
Here once the embattled farmers stood,
　And fired the shot heard round the world.

The foe long since in silence slept;
　Alike the conqueror silent sleeps;
And Time the ruined bridge has swept
　Down the dark stream which seaward creeps.

On this green bank, by this soft stream,
　We set to-day a votive stone;
That memory may their deed redeem,
　When, like our sires, our sons are gone.

Spirit, that made those heroes dare
　To die, and leave their children free,
Bid Time and Nature gently spare
　The shaft we raise to them and thee.

FRANCIS MILES FINCH

[1827–1907]

The Blue and the Gray

By the flow of the inland river,
  Whence the fleets of iron have fled,
Where the blades of the grave-grass quiver,
  Asleep are the ranks of the dead:—
    Under the sod and the dew
    Waiting the Judgment Day:—
    Under the one, the Blue;
    Under the other, the Gray.

These in the robings of glory,
  Those in the gloom of defeat,
All with the battle-blood gory,
  In the dusk of eternity meet:
    Under the sod and the dew,
    Waiting the Judgment Day:
    Under the laurel, the Blue,
    Under the willow, the Gray.

From the silence of sorrowful hours
  The desolate mourners go,

Lovingly laden with flowers,
  Alike for the friend and the foe:—
    Under the sod and the dew
    Waiting the Judgment Day:—
    Under the roses, the Blue;
    Under the lilies, the Gray.

So with an equal splendor,
  The morning sunrays fall,
With a touch impartially tender,
  On the blossoms blooming for all:
    Under the sod and the dew,
    Waiting the Judgment Day:
    Broidered with gold, the Blue,
    Mellowed with gold, the Gray.

So, when the summer calleth,
  On forest and field of grain,
With an equal murmur falleth
  The cooling drip of the rain:
    Under the sod and the dew,
      Waiting the Judgment Day:
    Wet with the rain, the Blue,
      Wet with the rain, the Gray.

Sadly, but not with upbraiding
  The generous deed was done.
In the storm of the years that are fading
  No braver battle was won:—
    Under the sod and the dew,
    Waiting the Judgment Day:—
    Under the blossoms, the Blue;
    Under the garlands, the Gray.

No more shall the war cry sever,
  Or the winding rivers be red:
They banish our anger forever
  When they laurel the graves of our dead!
  Under the sod and the dew,
    Waiting the Judgment Day:—
  Love and tears for the Blue;
Tears and love for the Gray.

ROBERT HAYDEN

[1913–1980]

Those Winter Sundays

Sundays too my father got up early
and put his clothes on in the blueblack cold,
then with cracked hands that ached
from labor in the weekday weather made
banked fires blaze. No one ever thanked him.

I'd wake and hear the cold splintering, breaking.
When the rooms were warm, he'd call,
and slowly I would rise and dress,
fearing the chronic angers of that house,

Speaking indifferently to him,
who had driven out the cold
and polished my good shoes as well.
What did I know, what did I know
of love's austere and lonely offices?

WILLIAM ERNEST HENLEY
[1849–1903]

Invictus

Out of the night that covers me,
   Black as the Pit from pole to pole,
I thank whatever gods may be
   For my unconquerable soul.

In the fell clutch of circumstance
   I have not winced nor cried aloud.
Under the bludgeonings of chance
   My head is bloody, but unbowed.

Beyond this place of wrath and tears
   Looms but the horror of the shade,
And yet the menace of the years
   Finds, and shall find me, unafraid.

It matters not how strait the gate,
   How charged with punishments the scroll,
I am the master of my fate:
   I am the captain of my soul.

GEORGE HERBERT

[1593–1633]

Love (III)

Love bade me welcome: yet my soul drew back,
      Guilty of dust and sin.
But quick-eyed Love, observing me grow slack
      From my first entrance in,
Drew nearer to me, sweetly questioning
      If I lacked anything.

"A guest," I answered, "worthy to be here":
      Love said, "You shall be he."
"I, the unkind, ungrateful? Ah, my dear,
      I cannot look on thee."
Love took my hand, and smiling did reply,
      "Who made the eyes but I?"

"Truth, Lord; but I have marred them; let my shame
      Go where it doth deserve."
"And know you not," says Love, "who bore the blame?"
      "My dear, then I will serve."
"You must sit down," says Love, "and taste my meat."
      So I did sit and eat.

GERARD MANLEY HOPKINS

[1844–1889]

Pied Beauty

Glory be to God for dappled things—
   For skies of couple-colour as a brinded cow;
      For rose-moles all in stipple upon trout that swim;
Fresh-firecoal chestnut-falls; finches' wings;
   Landscape plotted and pieced—fold, fallow, and plough;
      And áll trádes, their gear and tackle and trim.
All things counter, original, spare, strange;
   Whatever is fickle, freckled (who knows how?)
      With swift, slow; sweet, sour; adazzle, dim;
He fathers-forth whose beauty is past change:
         Praise him.

LANGSTON HUGHES

[1902–1967]

The Negro Speaks of Rivers

I've known rivers:
I've known rivers ancient as the world and older than the flow of human
   blood in human veins.

My soul has grown deep like the rivers.

I bathed in the Euphrates when dawns were young.
I built my hut near the Congo and it lulled me to sleep.
I looked upon the Nile and raised the pyramids above it.
I heard the singing of the Mississippi when Abe Lincoln went down to
   New Orleans, and I've seen its muddy bosom turn all golden in the
   sunset

I've known rivers:
Ancient, dusky rivers.

My soul has grown deep like the rivers.

BEN JONSON

[1572–1637]

To Celia

Drinke to me, onely, with thine eyes,
  And I will pledge with mine;
Or leave a kisse but in the cup,
  And Ile not looke for wine.
The thirst, that from the soule doth rise,
  Doth aske a drinke divine:
But might I of JOVE's *Nectar* sup,
  I would not change for thine.
I sent thee, late, a rosie wreath,
  Not so much honoring thee,
As giving it a hope, that there
  It could not withered bee.
But thou thereon did'st onely breath,
  And sent'st it back to mee:
Since when it growes, and smells, I sweare,
  Not of it selfe, but thee.

JAMES JOYCE
[1882–1941]

I hear an army charging upon the land

I hear an army charging upon the land,
   And the thunder of horses plunging, foam about their knees:
Arrogant, in black armour, behind them stand,
   Disdaining the reins, with fluttering whips, the charioteers.

They cry unto the night their battle-name:
   I moan in sleep when I hear afar their whirling laughter.
They cleave the gloom of dreams, a blinding flame,
   Clanging, clanging upon the heart as upon an anvil.

They come shaking in triumph their long, green hair:
   They come out of the sea and run shouting by the shore.
My heart, have you no wisdom thus to despair?
   My love, my love, my love, why have you left me alone?

RICHARD LOVELACE
[1618–1658]

To Althea, from Prison

When Love with unconfinéd wings
Hovers within my gates,
And my divine Althea brings
To whisper at the grates;
When I lie tangled in her hair
And fettered to her eye,
The birds that wanton in the air
Know no such liberty.

When flowing cups run swiftly round,
With no allaying Thames,
Our careless heads with roses bound,
Our hearts with loyal flames;
When thirsty grief in wine we steep,
When healths and draughts go free,
Fishes, that tipple in the deep,
Know no such liberty.

When, like committed linnets, I
With shriller throat shall sing

56

The sweetness, mercy, majesty,
And glories of my King;
When I shall voice aloud how good
He is, how great should be,
Enlargéd winds, that curl the flood,
Know no such liberty.

Stone walls do not a prison make,
Nor iron bars a cage;
Minds innocent and quiet take
That for an hermitage.
If I have freedom in my love,
And in my soul am free,
Angels alone, that soar above,
Enjoy such liberty.

ANDREW MARVELL

[1621–1678]

The Mower's Song

My mind was once the true survey
Of all these meadows fresh and gay,
And in the greenness of the grass
Did see its hopes as in a glass;
When Juliana came, and she
What I do to the grass, does to my thoughts and me.

But these, while I with sorrow pine,
Grew more luxuriant still and fine,
That not one blade of grass you spied,
But had a flower on either side;
When Juliana came, and she
What I do to the grass, does to my thoughts and me.

Unthankful meadows, could you so
A fellowship so true forgo,
And in your gaudy May-games meet,
While I lay trodden under feet?
When Juliana came, and she
What I do to the grass, does to my thoughts and me.

But what you in compassion ought,
Shall now by my revenge be wrought:
And flow'rs, and grass, and I and all,
Will in one common ruin fall.
For Juliana comes, and she
What I do to the grass, does to my thoughts and me.

And thus, ye meadows, which have been
Companions of my thoughts more green,
Shall now the heraldry become
With which I will adorn my tomb;
For Juliana comes, and she
What I do to the grass, does to my thoughts and me.

THOMAS NASHE

[1567–1601]

A Litany in Time of Plague

Adieu, farewell, earth's bliss;
This world uncertain is;
Fond are life's lustful joys;
Death proves them all but toys;
None from his darts can fly;
I am sick, I must die.
    Lord, have mercy on us!

Rich men, trust not in wealth,
Gold cannot buy you health;
Physic himself must fade.
All things to end are made,
The plague full swift goes by;
I am sick, I must die.
    Lord, have mercy on us!

Beauty is but a flower
Which wrinkles will devour;
Brightness falls from the air;
Queens have died young and fair;

Dust hath closed Helen's eye.
I am sick, I must die.
   Lord, have mercy on us!

Strength stoops unto the grave,
Worms feed on Hector brave;
Swords may not fight with fate,
Earth still holds ope her gate.
"Come, come!" the bells do cry.
I am sick, I must die.
   Lord, have mercy on us.

Wit with his wantonness
Tasteth death's bitterness;
Hell's executioner
Hath no ears for to hear
What vain art can reply.
I am sick, I must die.
   Lord, have mercy on us.

Haste, therefore, each degree,
To welcome destiny;
Heaven is our heritage,
Earth but a player's stage;
Mount we unto the sky.
I am sick, I must die.
   Lord, have mercy on us.

EDGAR ALLAN POE

[1809–1849]

To Helen

Helen, thy beauty is to me
　Like those Nicean barks of yore,
That gently, o'er a perfumed sea,
　The weary, way-worn wanderer bore
　To his own native shore.

On desperate seas long wont to roam,
　Thy hyacinth hair, thy classic face,
Thy Naiad airs have brought me home
　To the glory that was Greece
And the grandeur that was Rome.

Lo! in yon brilliant window-niche
　How statue-like I see thee stand!
　The agate lamp within thy hand,
Ah! Psyche from the regions which
　Are Holy Land!

SIR WALTER SCOTT
[1771–1832]

Coronach

He is gone on the mountain,
　He is lost to the forest,
Like a summer-dried fountain,
　When our need was the sorest.
The font reappearing
　From the raindrops shall borrow,
But to us comes no cheering,
　To Duncan no morrow!

The hand of the reaper
　Takes the ears that are hoary,
But the voice of the weeper
　Wails manhood in glory.
The autumn winds rushing
　Waft the leaves that are serest,
But our flower was in flushing
　When blighting was nearest.

Fleet foot on the correi,
    Sage counsel in cumber,
Red hand in the foray,
    How sound is thy slumber!

Like the dew on the mountain,
    Like the foam on the river,
Like the bubble on the fountain,
    Thou art gone, and for ever!

WILLIAM SHAKESPEARE

[1564–1616]

Blow, blow, thou winter wind

Blow, blow, thou winter wind,
Thou art not so unkind
   As man's ingratitude;
Thy tooth is not so keen,
Because thou art not seen,
   Although thy breath be rude.
Heigh-ho! sing, heigh-ho! unto the green holly:
Most friendship is feigning, most loving mere folly:
   Then, heigh-ho, the holly!
    This life is most jolly.

Freeze, freeze, thou bitter sky,
That dost not bite so nigh
   As benefits forgot:
Though thou the waters warp,
Thy sting is not so sharp
   As friend remembered not.
Heigh-ho! sing, . . .

WILLIAM SHAKESPEARE

[1564–1616]

When that I was and a little tiny boy

When that I was and a little tiny boy,
  With hey, ho, the wind and the rain,
A foolish thing was but a toy,
  For the rain it raineth every day.

But when I came to man's estate,
  With hey, ho, . . .
'Gainst knaves and thieves men shut their gate,
  For the rain, . . .

But when I came, alas! to wive,
  With hey, ho, . . .
By swaggering could I never thrive,
  For the rain, . . .

But when I came unto my beds,
  With hey, ho, . . .
With toss-pots still had drunken heads,
  For the rain, . . .

A great while ago the world begun,
    With hey, ho, . . .
But that's all one, our play is done,
    And we'll strive to please you every day.

ALFRED, LORD TENNYSON
[1809–1892]

The Splendor Falls

The splendor falls on castle walls
  And snowy summits old in story;
The long light shakes across the lakes,
  And the wild cataract leaps in glory.
Blow, bugle, blow, set the wild echoes flying,
Blow, bugle; answer, echoes, dying, dying, dying.

O, hark, O, hear! how thin and clear,
  And thinner, clearer, farther going!
O, sweet and far from cliff and scar
  The horns of Elfland faintly blowing!
Blow, let us hear the purple glens replying,
Blow, bugle; answer, echoes, dying, dying, dying.

O love, they die in yon rich sky,
  They faint on hill or field or river;
Our echoes roll from soul to soul,
  And grow forever and forever.
Blow, bugle, blow, set the wild echoes flying,
And answer, echoes, answer, dying, dying, dying.

ALFRED, LORD TENNYSON
[1809–1892]

FROM *In Memoriam*

Ring out, wild bells, to the wild sky,
　The flying cloud, the frosty light:
　The year is dying in the night;
Ring out, wild bells, and let him die.

Ring out the old, ring in the new,
　Ring, happy bells, across the snow:
　The year is going, let him go;
Ring out the false, ring in the true.

Ring out the grief that saps the mind,
　For those that here we see no more;
　Ring out the feud of rich and poor,
Ring in redress to all mankind.

Ring out a slowly dying cause,
　And ancient forms of party strife;
　Ring in the nobler modes of life,
With sweeter manners, purer laws.

Ring out the want, the care, the sin,
    The faithless coldness of the times;
    Ring out, ring out my mournful rhymes
But ring the fuller minstrel in.

Ring out false pride in place and blood,
    The civic slander and the spite;
    Ring in the love of truth and right,
Ring in the common love of good.

Ring out old shapes of foul disease;
    Ring out the narrowing lust of gold;
    Ring out the thousand wars of old,
Ring in the thousand years of peace.

Ring in the valiant man and free,
    The larger heart, the kindlier hand;
    Ring out the darkness of the land,
Ring in the Christ that is to be.

ALFRED, LORD TENNYSON
[1809–1892]

Tears, Idle Tears

Tears, idle tears, I know not what they mean,
Tears from the depth of some divine despair
Rise in the heart, and gather to the eyes,
In looking on the happy autumn-fields,
And thinking of the days that are no more.

Fresh as the first beam glittering on a sail,
That brings our friends up from the underworld,
Sad as the last which reddens over one
That sinks with all we love below the verge;
So sad, so fresh, the days that are no more.

Ah, sad and strange as in dark summer dawns
The earliest pipe of half-awakened birds
To dying ears, when unto dying eyes
The casement slowly grows a glimmering square;
So sad, so strange, the days that are no more.

Dear as remembered kisses after death,
And sweet as those by hopeless fancy feigned
On lips that are for others; deep as love,
Deep as first love, and wild with all regret;
O Death in Life, the days that are no more!

WALT WHITMAN

[1819–1892]

Song of Myself, #11

Twenty-eight young men bathe by the shore,
Twenty-eight young men and all so friendly;
Twenty-eight years of womanly life and all so lonesome.

She owns the fine house by the rise of the bank,
She hides handsome and richly drest aft the blinds of the window.

Which of the young men does she like the best?
Ah the homeliest of them is beautiful to her.

Where are you off to, lady? for I see you,
You splash in the water there, yet stay stock still in your room.

Dancing and laughing along the beach came the twenty-ninth bather,
The rest did not see her, but she saw them and loved them.

The beards of the young men glisten'd with wet, it ran from their long
   hair,
Little streams pass'd all over their bodies.

An unseen hand also pass'd over their bodies,
It descended trembling from their temples and ribs.

The young men float on their backs, their white bellies bulge to the sun, they do not ask who seizes fast to them,
They do not know who puffs and declines with pendant and bending arch,
They do not think whom they souse with spray.

WILLIAM CARLOS WILLIAMS
[1883–1963]

The Widow's Lament in Springtime

Sorrow is my own yard
where the new grass
flames as it has flamed
often before but not
with the cold fire
that closes round me this year.
Thirtyfive years
I lived with my husband.
The plumtree is white today
with masses of flowers.
Masses of flowers
load the cherry branches
and color some bushes
yellow and some red
but the grief in my heart
is stronger than they
for though they were my joy
formerly, today I notice them
and turned away forgetting.
Today my son told me

that in the meadows,
at the edge of the heavy woods
in the distance, he saw
trees of white flowers.
I feel that I would like
to go there
and fall into those flowers
and sink into the marsh near them.

WILLIAM WORDSWORTH

[1770–1850]

A slumber did my spirit seal

A slumber did my spirit seal;
  I had no human fears:
She seemed a thing that could not feel
  The touch of earthly years.

No motion has she now, no force;
  She neither hears nor sees;
Rolled round in earth's diurnal course,
  With rocks, and stones, and trees.

They flee from me

They flee from me, that sometime did me seek,
With naked foot stalking in my chamber.
I have seen them, gentle, tame, and meek,
That now are wild, and do not remember
That sometime they put themselves in danger
To take bread at my hand; and now they range,
Busily seeking with a continual change.

Thanked be Fortune it hath been otherwise,
Twenty times better; but once in special,
In thin array, after a pleasant guise,
When her loose gown from her shoulders did fall,
And she me caught in her arms long and small,
And therewith all sweetly did me kiss
And softly said, "Dear heart, how like you this?"

It was no dream, I lay broad waking.
But all is turned, thorough my gentleness,
Into a strange fashion of forsaking;
And I have leave to go, of her goodness,

And she also to use newfangleness.
But since that I so kindly am served,
I fain would know what she hath deserved.

WILLIAM BUTLER YEATS

[1865–1939]

The Cat and the Moon

The cat went here and there
And the moon spun round like a top,
And the nearest kin of the moon,
The creeping cat, looked up.
Black Minnaloushe stared at the moon,
For, wander and wail as he would,
The pure cold light in the sky
Troubled his animal blood.
Minnaloushe runs in the grass
Lifting his delicate feet.
Do you dance, Minnaloushe, do you dance?
When two close kindred meet,
What better than call a dance?
Maybe the moon may learn,
Tired of that courtly fashion,
A new dance turn.
Minnaloushe creeps through the grass
From moonlit place to place,
The sacred moon overhead
Has taken a new phase.

Does Minnaloushe know that his pupils
Will pass from change to change,
And that from round to crescent,
From crescent to round they range?
Minnaloushe creeps through the grass
Alone, important and wise,
And lifts to the changing moon
His changing eyes.

WILLIAM BUTLER YEATS

[1865 – 1939]

The Song of Wandering Aengus

I went out to the hazel wood,
Because a fire was in my head,
And cut and peeled a hazel wand,
And hooked a berry to a thread;
And when white moths were on the wing,
And moth-like stars were flickering out,
I dropped the berry in a stream
And caught a little silver trout.

When I had laid it on the floor
I went to blow the fire aflame,
But something rustled on the floor,
And some one called me by my name:
It had become a glimmering girl
With apple blossom in her hair
Who called me by my name and ran
And faded through the brightening air.

Though I am old with wandering
Through hollow lands and hilly lands,

I will find out where she has gone,
And kiss her lips and take her hands;
And walk among long dappled grass,
And pluck till time and times are done
The silver apples of the moon
The golden apples of the sun.

COUNSELS

LÉONIE ADAMS
[1 8 9 9 – 1 9 8 8]

April Mortality

Rebellion shook an ancient dust,
And bones, bleached dry of rottenness,
Said: Heart, be bitter still, nor trust
The earth, the sky, in their bright dress.

Heart, heart, dost thou not break to know
This anguish thou wilt bear alone?
We sang of it an age ago,
And traced it dimly upon stone.

With all the drifting race of men
Thou also art begot to mourn
That she is crucified again,
The lonely Beauty yet unborn.

And if thou dreamest to have won
Some touch of her in permanence,
'Tis the old cheating of the sun,
The intricate lovely play of sense.

Be bitter still, remember how
Four petals, when a little breath
Of wind made stir the pear-tree bough,
Blew delicately down to death.

Ecclesiastes 3:1–8

To every thing there is a season,
and a time to every purpose under the heaven:
A time to be born, and a time to die;
a time to plant, and a time to pluck up that which is planted;
A time to kill, and a time to heal;
a time to break down, and a time to build up;
A time to weep, and a time to laugh;
a time to mourn, and a time to dance;
A time to cast away stones, and a time to gather stones together;
a time to embrace, and a time to refrain from embracing;
A time to get, and a time to lose;
a time to keep, and a time to cast away;
A time to rend, and a time to sew;
a time to keep silence, and a time to speak;
A time to love, and a time to hate;
a time of war, and a time of peace.

RALPH WALDO EMERSON

[1803–1882]

Brahma

If the red slayer think he slays,
　Or if the slain think he is slain,
They know not well the subtle ways
　I keep, and pass, and turn again.

Far or forgot to me is near;
　Shadow and sunlight are the same;
The vanished gods to me appear;
　And one to me are shame and fame.

They reckon ill who leave me out;
　When me they fly, I am the wings;
I am the doubter and the doubt;
　And I the hymn the Brahmin sings.

The strong gods pine for my abode,
　And pine in vain the sacred Seven,
But thou, meek lover of the good!
　Find me, and turn thy back on heaven.

EDWARD FITZGERALD

[1809 – 1883]

FROM *The Rubáiyát of Omar Khayyám*

I: 1–3, V: 12–15, 19–24, 71–72

1

Wake! For the Sun, who scattered into flight
The Stars before him from the Field of Night,
    Drives Night along with them from Heav'n and strikes
The Sultán's Turret with a Shaft of Light.

2

Before the phantom of False morning died,
Methought a Voice within the Tavern cried,
    "When all the Temple is prepared within,
Why nods the drowsy Worshiper outside?"

3

And, as the Cock crew, those who stood before
The Tavern shouted—"Open, then, the Door!
    You know how little while we have to stay,
And, once departed, may return no more."

12

A Book of Verses underneath the Bough,
A Jug of Wine, a Loaf of Bread—and Thou
    Beside me singing in the Wilderness—
Oh, Wilderness were Paradise enow!

13

Some for the Glories of This World; and some
Sigh for the Prophet's Paradise to come;
    Ah, take the Cash, and let the Credit go,
Nor heed the rumble of a distant Drum!

14

Look to the blowing Rose about us—"Lo,
Laughing," she says, "into the world I blow,
    At once the silken tassel of my Purse
Tear, and its Treasure on the Garden throw."

15

And those who husbanded the Golden Grain,
And those who flung it to the winds like Rain,
    Alike to no such aureate Earth are turned
As, buried once, Men want dug up again.

19

I sometimes think that never blows so red
The Rose as where some buried Caesar bled;
    That every Hyacinth the Garden wears
Dropped in her Lap from some once lovely Head.

And this reviving Herb whose tender Green
Fledges the River-Lip on which we lean—
    Ah, lean upon it lightly! for who knows
From what once lovely Lip it springs unseen!

Ah, my Belovéd, fill the Cup that clears
Today of past Regrets and future Fears:
    Tomorrow!—Why, Tomorrow I may be
Myself with Yesterday's Sev'n thousand Years.

For some we loved, the loveliest and the best
That from his Vintage rolling Time hath pressed,
    Have drunk their Cup a Round or two before,
And one by one crept silently to rest.

And we, that now make merry in the Room
They left, and Summer dresses in new bloom,
    Ourselves must we beneath the Couch of Earth
Descend—ourselves to make a Couch—for whom?

Ah, make the most of what we yet may spend,
Before we too into the Dust descend;
    Dust into Dust, and under Dust to lie,
Sans Wine, sans Song, sans Singer, and—sans End!

71

The Moving Finger writes, and, having writ,
Moves on; nor all your Piety nor Wit
   Shall lure it back to cancel half a Line,
Nor all your Tears wash out a Word of it.

72

And that inverted Bowl they call the Sky,
Whereunder crawling cooped we live and die,
   Lift not your hands to *It* for help—for It
As impotently moves as you or I.

GEORGE HERBERT

[1593–1633]

The World

Love built a stately house, where Fortune came,
And spinning fancies, she was heard to say
That her fine cobwebs did support the frame,
Whereas they were supported by the same;
But Wisdom quickly swept them all away.

Then Pleasure came, who, liking not the fashion,
Began to make balconies, terraces,
Till she had weakened all by alteration;
But reverend laws, and many a proclamation
Reformèd all at length with menaces.

Then entered Sin, and with that sycamore
Whose leaves first sheltered man from drought and dew,
Working and winding slily evermore,
The inward walls and summers cleft and tore;
But Grace shored these, and cut that as it grew.

Then Sin combined with death in a firm band,
To raze the building to the very floor;
Which they effected,—none could them withstand;
But Love and Grace took Glory by the hand,
And built a braver palace than before.

ROBERT HERRICK

[1591–1674]

To the Virgins, to Make Much of Time

Gather ye rosebuds while ye may,
　Old time is still a-flying;
And this same flower that smiles today
　Tomorrow will be dying.

The glorious lamp of heaven, the sun,
　The higher he's a-getting,
The sooner will his race be run,
　And nearer he's to setting.

That age is best which is the first,
　When youth and blood are warmer;
But being spent, the worse, and worst
　Times still succeed the former.

Then be not coy, but use your time,
　And, while ye may, go marry;
For, having lost but once your prime,
　You may forever tarry.

A. E. HOUSMAN

[1859–1936]

To an Athlete Dying Young

The time you won your town the race
We chaired you through the market-place;
Man and boy stood cheering by,
And home we brought you shoulder-high.

To-day, the road all runners come,
Shoulder-high we bring you home,
And set you at your threshold down,
Townsman of a stiller town.

Smart lad, to slip betimes away
From fields where glory does not stay
And early though the laurel grows
It withers quicker than the rose.

Eyes the shady night has shut
Cannot see the record cut,
And silence sounds no worse than cheers
After earth has stopped the ears:

Now you would not swell the rout
Of lads that wore their honours out,
Runners whom renown outran
And the name died before the man.

So set, before its echoes fade,
The fleet foot on the sill of shade,
And hold to the low lintel up
The still-defended challenge-cup.

And round that early-laurelled head
Will flock to gaze the strengthless dead
And find unwithered on its curls
The garland briefer than a girl's.

RUDYARD KIPLING

[1865–1936]

If

If you can keep your head when all about you
   Are losing theirs and blaming it on you;
If you can trust yourself when all men doubt you,
   But make allowance for their doubting too;
If you can wait and not be tired by waiting,
   Or, being lied about, don't deal in lies,
Or, being hated, don't give way to hating,
   And yet don't look too good, nor talk too wise;

If you can dream—and not make dreams your master;
   If you can think—and not make thoughts your aim;
If you can meet with triumph and disaster
   And treat those two impostors just the same;
If you can bear to hear the truth you've spoken
   Twisted by knaves to make a trap for fools,
Or watch the things you gave your life to broken,
   And stoop and build 'em up with wornout tools;

If you can make one heap of all your winnings
   And risk it on one turn of pitch-and-toss,

And lose, and start again at your beginnings
   And never breathe a word about your loss;
If you can force your heart and nerve and sinew
   To serve your turn long after they are gone,
And so hold on when there is nothing in you
   Except the Will which says to them: "Hold on";

If you can talk with crowds and keep your virtue,
   Or walk with kings—nor lose the common touch;
If neither foes nor loving friends can hurt you;
   If all men count with you, but none too much;
If you can fill the unforgiving minute
   With sixty seconds' worth of distance run—
Yours is the Earth and everything that's in it,
   And—which is more—you'll be a Man, my son!

CHRISTINA ROSSETTI

[1830–1894]

Up-Hill

Does the road wind up-hill all the way?
  Yes, to the very end.
Will the day's journey take the whole long day?
  From morn to night, my friend.

But is there for the night a resting-place?
  A roof for when the slow dark hours begin.
May not the darkness hide it from my face?
  You cannot miss that inn.

Shall I meet other wayfarers at night?
  Those who have gone before.
Then must I knock, or call when just in sight?
  They will not keep you standing at that door.

Shall I find comfort, travel-sore and weak?
  Of labour you shall find the sum.
Will there be beds for me and all who seek?
  Yea, beds for all who come.

DYLAN THOMAS

[1914–1953]

Do not go gentle into that good night

Do not go gentle into that good night,
Old age should burn and rave at close of day;
Rage, rage against the dying of the light.

Though wise men at their end know dark is right,
Because their words had forked no lightning they
Do not go gentle into that good night.

Good men, the last wave by, crying how bright
Their frail deeds might have danced in a green bay,
Rage, rage against the dying of the light.

Wild men who caught and sang the sun in flight,
And learn, too late, they grieved it on its way,
Do not go gentle into that good night.

Grave men, near death, who see with blinding sight
Blind eyes could blaze like meteors and be gay,
Rage, rage against the dying of the light.

And you, my father, there on the sad height,
Curse, bless, me now with your fierce tears, I pray.
Do not go gentle into that good night.
Rage, rage against the dying of the light.

EDMUND WALLER

[1606–1687]

Go, lovely rose!

Go, lovely rose!
Tell her that wastes her time and me
That now she knows,
When I resemble her to thee,
How sweet and fair she seems to be.

Tell her that's young,
And shuns to have her graces spied,
That hadst thou sprung
In deserts, where no men abide,
Thou must have uncommended died.

Small is the worth
Of beauty from the light retired;
Bid her come forth,
Suffer herself to be desired,
And not blush so to be admired.

Then die! that she
The common fate of all things rare
    May read in thee;
How small a part of time they share
That are so wondrous sweet and fair!

ELINOR WYLIE

[1 8 8 5 – 1 9 2 8]

The Eagle and the Mole

Avoid the reeking herd,
Shun the polluted flock,
Live like that stoic bird,
The eagle of the rock.

The huddled warmth of crowds
Begets and fosters hate;
He keeps, above the clouds,
His cliff inviolate.

When flocks are folded warm,
And herds to shelter run,
He sails above the storm,
He stares into the sun.

If in the eagle's track
Your sinews cannot leap,
Avoid the lathered pack,
Turn from the steaming sheep.

If you would keep your soul
From spotted sight or sound,
Live like the velvet mole;
Go burrow underground.

And there hold intercourse
With roots of trees and stones,
With rivers at their source,
And disembodied bones.

WILLIAM BUTLER YEATS

[1865–1939]

The Second Coming

Turning and turning in the widening gyre
The falcon cannot hear the falconer;
Things fall apart; the center cannot hold;
Mere anarchy is loosed upon the world,
The blood-dimmed tide is loosed, and everywhere
The ceremony of innocence is drowned;
The best lack all conviction, while the worst
Are full of passionate intensity.

Surely some revelation is at hand;
Surely the Second Coming is at hand;
The Second Coming! Hardly are those words out
When a vast image out of *Spiritus Mundi*
Troubles my sight: somewhere in sands of the desert
A shape with lion body and the head of a man,
A gaze blank and pitiless as the sun,
Is moving its slow thighs, while all about it
Reel shadows of the indignant desert birds.

The darkness drops again; but now I know
That twenty centuries of stony sleep
Were vexed to nightmare by a rocking cradle,
And what rough beast, its hour come round at last,
Slouches towards Bethlehem to be born?

TALES

Lord Randall

"Oh where ha'e ye been, Lord Randall my son?
O where ha'e ye been, my handsome young man?"
  "I ha'e been to the wild wood: mother, make my bed soon,
  For I'm weary wi' hunting, and fain wald lie down."

"Where gat ye your dinner, Lord Randall my son?
Where gat ye your dinner, my handsome young man?"
  "I dined wi' my true love; mother, make my bed soon,
  For I'm weary wi' hunting, and fain wald lie down."

"What gat ye to your dinner, Lord Randall my son?
What gat ye to your dinner, my handsome young man?"
  "I gat eels boiled in broo: mother, make my bed soon,
  For I'm weary wi' hunting, and fain wald lie down."

"What became of your bloodhounds, Lord Randall my son?
What became of your bloodhounds, my handsome young man?"
  "O they swelled and they died: mother, make my bed soon,
  For I'm weary wi' hunting, and fain wald lie down."

"O I fear ye are poisoned, Lord Randall my son!
O I fear ye are poisoned, my handsome young man!"
"O yes, I am poisoned: mother, make my bed soon,
For I'm sick at the heart, and I fain wald lie down."

My Last Duchess

Ferrara

That's my last Duchess painted on the wall,
Looking as if she were alive. I call
That piece a wonder, now; Frà Pandolf's hands
Worked busily a day, and there she stands.
Will 't please you sit and look at her? I said
"Frà Pandolf" by design, for never read
Strangers like you that pictured countenance,
The depth and passion of its earnest glance,
But to myself they turned (since none puts by
The curtain I have drawn for you, but I)
And seemed as they would ask me, if they durst,
How such a glance came there; so, not the first
Are you to turn and ask thus. Sir, 'twas not
Her husband's presence only, called that spot
Of joy into the Duchess' cheek; perhaps
Frà Pandolf chanced to say, "Her mantle laps
Over my lady's wrist too much," or "Paint
Must never hope to reproduce the faint

Half-flush that dies along her throat." Such stuff
Was courtesy, she thought, and cause enough
For calling up that spot of joy. She had
A heart—how shall I say?—too soon made glad,
Too easily impressed; she liked whate'er
She looked on, and her looks went everywhere.
Sir, 'twas all one! My favor at her breast,
The dropping of the daylight in the West,
The bough of cherries some officious fool
Broke in the orchard for her, the white mule
She rode with round the terrace—all and each
Would draw from her alike the approving speech,
Or blush, at least. She thanked men,—good! but thanked
Somehow—I know not how—as if she ranked
My gift of a nine-hundred-years-old name
With anybody's gift. Who'd stoop to blame
This sort of trifling? Even had you skill
In speech—which I have not—to make your will
Quite clear to such an one, and say "Just this
Or that in you disgusts me; here you miss,
Or there exceed the mark"—and if she let
Herself be lessoned so, nor plainly set
Her wits to yours, forsooth, and made excuse—
E'en then would be some stooping; and I choose
Never to stoop. Oh sir, she smiled, no doubt,
Whene'er I passed her; but who passed without
Much the same smile? This grew; I gave commands;
Then all smiles-stopped together. There she stands
As if alive. Will 't please you rise? We'll meet
The company below, then. I repeat,
The Count your master's known munificence
Is ample warrant that no just pretense
Of mine for dowry will be disallowed;

Though his fair daughter's self, as I avowed
At starting, is my object. Nay, we'll go
Together down, sir. Notice Neptune, though,
Taming a sea-horse, thought a rarity,
Which Claus of Innsbruck cast in bronze for me!

LEWIS CARROLL

(CHARLES LUTWIDGE DODGSON)

[1832–1898]

Jabberwocky

'Twas brillig, and the slithy toves
   Did gyre and gimble in the wabe:
All mimsy were the borogoves,
   And the mome raths outgrabe.

"Beware the Jabberwock, my son!
   The jaws that bite, the claws that catch!
Beware the Jubjub bird, and shun
   The frumious Bandersnatch!"

He took his vorpal sword in hand:
   Long time the manxome foe he sought—
So rested he by the Tumtum tree,
   And stood awhile in thought.

And, as in uffish thought he stood,
   The Jabberwock, with eyes of flame,
Came whiffling through the tulgey wood,
   And burbled as it came!

One, two! One, two! And through and through
    The vorpal blade went snicker-snack!
He left it dead, and with its head
    He went galumphing back.

"And hast thou slain the Jabberwock?
    Come to my arms, my beamish boy!
O frabjous day! Callooh! Callay!"
He chortled in his joy.

'Twas brillig, and the slithy toves
    Did gyre and gimble in the wabe:
All mimsy were the borogoves,
    And the mome raths outgrabe.

65

SAMUEL TAYLOR COLERIDGE

[1772–1834]

Kubla Khan

Or a Vision in a Dream. A Fragment

In Xanadu did Kubla Khan
A stately pleasure dome decree:
Where Alph, the sacred river, ran
Through caverns measureless to man
   Down to a sunless sea.
So twice five miles of fertile ground
With walls and towers were girdled round:
And there were gardens bright with sinuous rills,
Where blossomed many an incense-bearing tree;
And here were forests ancient as the hills,
Enfolding sunny spots of greenery.

But oh! that deep romantic chasm which slanted
Down the green hill athwart a cedarn cover!
A savage place! as holy and enchanted
As e'er beneath a waning moon was haunted
By woman wailing for her demon lover!
And from this chasm, with ceaseless turmoil seething,

As if this earth in fast thick pants were breathing,
A mighty fountain momently was forced:
Amid whose swift half-intermitted burst
Huge fragments vaulted like rebounding hail,
Or chaffy grain beneath the thresher's flail:
And 'mid these dancing rocks at once and ever
It flung up momently the sacred river.
Five miles meandering with a mazy motion
Through wood and dale the sacred river ran,
Then reached the caverns measureless to man,
And sank in tumult to a lifeless ocean:
And 'mid this tumult Kubla heard from far
Ancestral voices prophesying war!

    The shadow of the dome of pleasure
    Floated midway on the waves;
    Where was heard the mingled measure
    From the fountains and the caves.
It was a miracle of rare device,
A sunny pleasure dome with caves of ice!

    A damsel with a dulcimer
    In a vision once I saw:
    It was an Abyssinian maid,
    And on her dulcimer she played,
    Singing of Mount Abora.
Could I revive within me
Her symphony and song,
To such a deep delight 'twould win me,
That with music loud and long,
I would build that dome in air,
That sunny dome! those caves of ice!
And all who heard should see them there,

And all should cry, Beware! Beware!
His flashing eyes, his floating hair!
Weave a circle round him thrice,
And close your eyes with holy dread,
For he on honey-dew hath fed,
And drunk the milk of Paradise.

66

E. E. CUMMINGS
[1884–1962]

anyone lived in a pretty how town

anyone lived in a pretty how town
(with up so floating many bells down)
spring summer autumn winter
he sang his didn't he danced his did.

Women and men (both little and small)
cared for anyone not at all
they sowed their isn't they reaped their same
sun moon stars rain

children guessed (but only a few
and down they forgot as up they grew
autumn winter spring summer)
that noone loved him more by more

when by now and tree by leaf
she laughed his joy she cried his grief
bird by snow and stir by still
anyone's any was all to her

someones married their everyones
laughed their cryings and did their dance
(sleep wake hope and then) they
said their nevers they slept their dream

stars rain sun moon
(and only the snow can begin to explain
how children are apt to forget to remember
with up so floating many bells down)

one day anyone died i guess
(and noone stooped to kiss his face)
busy folk buried them side by side
little by little and was by was

all by all and deep by deep
and more by more they dream their sleep
noone and anyone earth by april
wish by spirit and if by yes.

Women and men (both dong and ding)
summer autumn winter spring
reaped their sowing and went their came
sun moon stars rain

ROBERT FROST

[1874–1963]

The Road Not Taken

Two roads diverged in a yellow wood,
And sorry I could not travel both
And be one traveler, long I stood
And looked down one as far as I could
To where it bent in the undergrowth;

Then took the other, as just as fair,
And having perhaps the better claim,
Because it was grassy and wanted wear;
Though as for that, the passing there
Had worn them really about the same,

And both that morning equally lay
In leaves no step had trodden black.
Oh, I kept the first for another day!
Yet knowing how way leads on to way,
I doubted if I should ever come back.

I shall be telling this with a sigh
Somewhere ages and ages hence:
Two roads diverged in a wood, and I—
I took the one less traveled by,
And that has made all the difference.

THOMAS GRAY

[1716–1771]

Ode on the death of a favorite cat,
drowned in a tub of goldfishes

Twas on a lofty vase's side,
Where China's gayest art had dyed
  The azure flowers that blow;
Demurest of the tabby kind,
The pensive Selima, reclined,
  Gazed on the lake below.

Her conscious tail her joy declared;
The fair round face, the snowy beard,
  The velvet of her paws,
Her coat, that with the tortoise vies,
Her ears of jet, and emerald eyes,
  She saw; and purred applause.

Still had she gazed; but 'midst the tide
Two angel forms were seen to glide,
  The genii of the stream:

Their scaly armor's Tyrian hue
Through richest purple to the view
    Betrayed a golden gleam.

The hapless nymph with wonder saw:
A whisker first and then a claw,
    With many an ardent wish,
She stretched in vain to reach the prize.
What female heart can gold despise?
    What cat's averse to fish?

Presumptuous maid! with looks intent
Again she stretched, again she bent,
    Nor knew the gulf between.
(Malignant Fate sat by and smiled)
The slippery verge her feet beguiled,
    She tumbled headlong in.

Eight times emerging from the flood
She mewed to every watery god,
    Some speedy aid to send.
No dolphin came, no Nereid stirred;
Nor cruel Tom, nor Susan heard;
    A favorite has no friend!

From hence, ye beauties, undeceived,
Know, one false step is ne'er retrieved,
    And be with caution bold.
Not all that tempts your wandering eyes
And heedless hearts, is lawful prize;
    Nor all that glisters, gold.

THOMAS HARDY

[1840–1928]

The Oxen

Christmas Eve, and twelve of the clock.
　"Now they are all on their knees,"
An elder said as we sat in a flock
　By the embers in hearthside ease.

We pictured the meek mild creatures where
　They dwelt in their strawy pen,
Nor did it occur to one of us there
　To doubt they were kneeling then.

So fair a fancy few would weave
　In these years! Yet, I feel,
If someone said on Christmas Eve,
　"Come; see the oxen kneel,

"In the lonely barton by yonder coomb
　Our childhood used to know,"
I should go with him in the gloom,
　Hoping it might be so.

[1795–1821]

La Belle Dame sans Merci

O what can ail thee, Knight at arms,
   Alone and palely loitering?
The sedge has withered from the Lake
   And no birds sing!

O what can ail thee, Knight at arms,
   So haggard, and so woebegone?
The squirrel's granary is full
   And the harvest's done.

I see a lily on thy brow
   With anguish moist and fever dew,
And on thy cheeks a fading rose
   Fast withereth too.

"I met a Lady in the Meads,"
   Full beautiful, a faery's child,
Her hair was long, her foot was light
   And her eyes were wild.

"I made a Garland for her head,
    And bracelets too, and fragrant Zone;
She looked at me as she did love
    And made sweet moan.

"I set her on my pacing steed
    And nothing else saw all day long,
For sidelong would she bend and sing
    A faery's song.

"She found me roots of relish sweet,
    And honey wild, and manna dew,
And sure in language strange she said
    'I love thee true.'

"She took me to her elfin grot
    And there she wept and sighed full sore,
And there I shut her wild wild eyes
    With kisses four.

"And there she lulléd me asleep,
    And there I dreamed, Ah Woe betide!
The latest dream I ever dreamt
    On the cold hill side.

"I saw pale Kings, and Princes too,
    Pale warriors, death-pale were they all;
They cried, 'La belle dame sans merci
    Hath thee in thrall!'

"I saw their starved lips in the gloam
    With horrid warning gapéd wide,
And I awoke, and found me here
    On the cold hill's side.

"And this is why I sojourn here,
　　Alone and palely loitering;
Though the sedge is withered from the Lake
　　And no birds sing."

EDWARD LEAR

[1812–1888]

The Owl and the Pussy-cat

The Owl and the Pussy-cat went to sea
  In a beautiful pea-green boat,
They took some honey, and plenty of money,
  Wrapped up in a five-pound note.
The Owl looked up to the stars above,
  And sang to a small guitar,
"O lovely Pussy! O Pussy, my love,
  What a beautiful Pussy you are,
    You are,
    You are!
  What a beautiful Pussy you are!"

Pussy said to the Owl, "You elegant fowl!
  How charmingly sweet you sing!
O let us be married! too long we have tarried:
  But what shall we do for a ring?"
They sailed away, for a year and a day,
  To the land where the Bong-tree grows
And there in a wood a Piggy-wig stood
  With a ring at the end of his nose,

His nose,
His nose,
With a ring at the end of his nose.

"Dear Pig, are you willing to sell for one shilling
    Your ring?" Said the Piggy, "I will."
So they took it away, and were married next day
    By the Turkey who lives on the hill.
They dined on mince, and slices of quince,
    Which they ate with a runcible spoon
And hand in hand, on the edge of the sand,
    They danced by the light of the moon,
        The moon,
        The moon,
    They danced by the light of the moon.

EDWIN ARLINGTON ROBINSON

[1869–1935]

Richard Cory

Whenever Richard Cory went down town,
We people on the pavement looked at him:
He was a gentleman from sole to crown,
Clean favored and imperially slim.

And he was always quietly arrayed,
And he was always human when he talked,
But still he fluttered pulses when he said,
"Good-morning," and he glittered when he walked.

And he was rich—yes, richer than a king—
And admirably schooled in every grace:
In fine, we thought that he was everything
To make us wish that we were in his place.

So on we worked, and waited for the light,
And went without the meat and cursed the bread;
And Richard Cory, one calm summer night,
Went home and put a bullet through his head.

An Apple Gathering

I plucked pink blossoms from mine apple-tree
 And wore them all that evening in my hair:
Then in due season when I went to see
 I found no apples there.

With dangling basket all along the grass
 As I had come I went the selfsame track:
My neighbours mocked me while they saw me pass
 So empty-handed back.

Lilian and Lilias smiled in trudging by,
 Their heaped-up basket teased me like a jeer;
Sweet-voiced they sang beneath the sunset sky,
 Their mother's home was near.

Plump Gertrude passed me with her basket full,
 A stronger hand than hers helped it along;
A voice talked with her through the shadows cool
 More sweet to me than song.

Ah Willie, Willie, was my love less worth
    Than apples with their green leaves piled above?
I counted rosiest apples on the earth
    Of far less worth than love.

So once it was with me you stooped to talk
    Laughing and listening in this very lane:
To think that by this way we used to walk
    We shall not walk again!

I let my neighbours pass me, ones and twos
    And groups; the latest said the night grew chill,
And hastened: but I loitered, while the dews
    Fell fast I loitered still.

DANTE GABRIEL ROSSETTI

[1828 – 1882]

The Woodspurge

The wind flapped loose, the wind was still,
Shaken out dead from tree and hill:
I had walked on at the wind's will,—
I sat now, for the wind was still.

Between my knees my forehead was,—
My lips, drawn in, said not Alas!
My hair was over in the grass,
My naked ears heard the day pass.

My eyes, wide open, had the run
Of some ten weeds to fix upon;
Among those few, out of the sun,
The woodspurge flowered, three cups in one.

From perfect grief there need not be
Wisdom or even memory:
One thing then learnt remains to me,—
The woodspurge has a cup of three.

All the world's a stage

All the world's a stage,
And all the men and women merely players;
They have their exits and their entrances,
And one man in his time plays many parts,
His acts being seven ages. At first, the infant,
Mewling and puking in the nurse's arms.
Then the whining schoolboy, with his satchel
And shining morning face, creeping like snail
Unwillingly to school. And then the lover,
Sighing like furnace, with a woeful ballad
Made to his mistress' eyebrow. Then a soldier,
Full of strange oaths and bearded like the pard,
Jealous in honor, sudden and quick in quarrel,
Seeking the bubble reputation
Even in the cannon's mouth. And then the justice,
In fair round belly with good capon lined,
With eyes severe and beard of formal cut,
Full of wise saws and modern instances;
And so he plays his part. The sixth age shifts
Into the lean and slippered pantaloon,

With spectacles on nose and pouch on side;
His youthful hose, well saved, a world too wide
For his shrunk shank, and his big manly voice,
Turning again toward childish treble, pipes
And whistles in his sound. Last scene of all,
That ends this strange eventful history,
Is second childishness and mere oblivion,
Sans teeth, sans eyes, sans taste, sans everything.

ERNEST LAWRENCE THAYER

[1863–1940]

Casey at the Bat

The outlook wasn't brilliant for the Mudville nine that day:
The score stood four to two, with but one inning more to play,
And then when Cooney died at first, and Barrows did the same,
A pall-like silence fell upon the patrons of the game.

A straggling few got up to go in deep despair. The rest
Clung to that hope which springs eternal in the human breast;
They thought, "If only Casey could but get a whack at that—
We'd put up even money now, with Casey at the bat."

But Flynn preceded Casey, as did also Jimmy Blake,
And the former was a hoodoo, while the latter was a cake;
So upon that stricken multitude grim melancholy sat,
For there seemed but little chance of Casey getting to the bat.

But Flynn let drive a single, to the wonderment of all,
And Blake, the much despisèd, tore the cover off the ball;
And when the dust had lifted, and men saw what had occurred,
There was Jimmy safe at second and Flynn a-hugging third.

Then from five thousand throats and more there rose a lusty yell;
It rumbled through the valley, it rattled in the dell;
It pounded on the mountain and recoiled upon the flat,
For Casey, mighty Casey, was advancing to the bat.

There was ease in Casey's manner as he stepped into his place;
There was pride in Casey's bearing and a smile lit Casey's face.
And when, responding to the cheers, he lightly doffed his hat,
No stranger in the crowd could doubt 'twas Casey at the bat.

Ten thousand eyes were on him as he rubbed his hands with dirt;
Five thousand tongues applauded when he wiped them on his shirt;
Then while the writhing pitcher ground the ball into his hip,
Defiance flashed in Casey's eye, a sneer curled Casey's lip.

And now the leather-covered sphere came hurtling through the air,
And Casey stood a-watching it in haughty grandeur there.
Close by the sturdy batsman the ball unheeded sped—
"That ain't my style," said Casey. "Strike one!" the umpire said.

From the benches, black with people, there went up a muffled roar,
Like the beating of the storm-waves on a stern and distant shore;
"Kill him! Kill the umpire!" shouted some one on the stand;
And it's likely they'd have killed him had not Casey raised his hand.

With a smile of Christian charity great Casey's visage shone;
He stilled the rising tumult; he bade the game go on;
He signaled to the pitcher, and once more the dun sphere flew;
But Casey still ignored it and the umpire said, "Strike two!"

"Fraud!" cried the maddened thousands, and echo answered "Fraud!"
But one scornful look from Casey and the audience was awed.
They saw his face grow stern and cold, they saw his muscles strain,
And they knew that Casey wouldn't let that ball go by again.

The sneer has fled from Casey's lip, his teeth are clenched in hate;
He pounds with cruel violence his bat upon the plate.
And now the pitcher holds the ball, and now he lets it go,
And now the air is shattered by the force of Casey's blow.

Oh, somewhere in this favored land the sun is shining bright;
The band is playing somewhere, and somewhere hearts are light,
And somewhere men are laughing, and little children shout;
But there is no joy in Mudville—great Casey has struck out.

EDWARD THOMAS
[1878–1917]

Adlestrop

Yes. I remember Adlestrop—
The name, because one afternoon
Of heat the express-train drew up there
Unwontedly. It was late June.

The steam hissed. Someone cleared his throat.
No one left and no one came
On the bare platform. What I saw
Was Adlestrop—only the name

And willows, willow-herb, and grass,
And meadowsweet, and haycocks dry,
No whit less still and lonely fair
Than the high cloudlets in the sky.

And for that minute a blackbird sang
Close by, and round him, mistier,
Farther and farther, all the birds
Of Oxfordshire and Gloucestershire.

FROM *Snow-Bound*

11: 1–40, 116–154

The sun that brief December day
Rose cheerless over hills of gray,
And, darkly circled, gave at noon
A sadder light than waning moon.
Slow tracing down the thickening sky
Its mute and ominous prophecy,
A portent seeming less than threat,
It sank from sight before it set.
A chill no coat, however stout,
Of homespun stuff could quite shut out,
    A hard, dull bitterness of cold,
That checked, mid-vein, the circling race
Of life-blood in the sharpened face,
    The coming of the snow-storm told.
The wind blew east: we heard the roar
Of Ocean on his wintry shore,
And felt the strong pulse throbbing there
Beat with low rhythm our inland air.

Meanwhile we did our nightly chores,—
Brought in the wood from out of doors,
Littered the stalls, and from the mows
Raked down the herd's-grass for the cows;
Heard the horse whinnying for his corn;
And, sharply clashing horn on horn,
Impatient down the stanchion rows
The cattle shake their walnut bows;
While, peering from his early perch
Upon the scaffold's pole of birch,
The cock his crested helmet bent
And down his querulous challenge sent.

Unwarmed by any sunset light
The gray day darkened into night,
A night made hoary with the swarm
And whirl-dance of the blinding storm,
As zigzag, wavering to and fro
Crossed and recrossed the wingèd snow:
And ere the early bed-time came
The white drift piled the window-frame,
And through the glass the clothes-line posts
Looked in like tall and sheeted ghosts.

❧

As night drew on, and, from the crest
Of wooded knolls that ridged the west,
The sun, a snow-blown traveller, sank
From sight beneath the smothering bank,
We piled, with care, our nightly stack
Of wood against the chimney-back,—
The oaken log, green, huge, and thick,

And on its top the stout back-stick;
The knotty forestick laid apart,
And filled between with curious art
The ragged brush; then, hovering near,
We watched the first red blaze appear,
Heard the sharp crackle, caught the gleam
On whitewashed wall and sagging beam,
Until the old, rude-furnished room
Burst, flower-like, into rosy bloom;
While radiant with a mimic flame
Outside the sparkling drift became,
And through the bare-boughed lilac-tree
Our own warm hearth seemed blazing free.
The crane and pendent trammels showed,
The Turks' heads on the andirons glowed;
While childish fancy, prompt to tell
The meaning of the miracle,
Whispered the old rhyme: "Under the tree,
When fire outdoors burns merrily,
There the witches are making tea."
The moon above the eastern wood
Shone at its full; the hill-range stood
Transfigured in the silver flood,
Its blown snows flashing cold and keen,
Dead white, save where some sharp ravine
Took shadow, or the sombre green
Of hemlocks turned to pitchy black
Against the whiteness at their back.
For such a world and such a night
Most fitting that unwarming light,
Which only seemed where'er it fell
To make the coldness visible.

MEDITATIONS

MATTHEW ARNOLD
[1 8 2 2 – 1 8 8 8]

Dover Beach

The sea is calm tonight.
The tide is full, the moon lies fair
Upon the straits; on the French coast the light
Gleams and is gone; the cliffs of England stand,
Glimmering and vast, out in the tranquil bay.
Come to the window, sweet is the night-air!
Only, from the long line of spray
Where the sea meets the moon-blanched land,

Listen! you hear the grating roar
Of pebbles which the waves draw back, and fling,
At their return, up the high strand,
Begin, and cease, and then again begin,
With tremulous cadence slow, and bring
The eternal note of sadness in.

Sophocles long ago
Heard it on the Aegean, and it brought
Into his mind the turbid ebb and flow

Of human misery; we
Find also in the sound a thought,
Hearing it by this distant northern sea.

The Sea of Faith
Was once, too, at the full, and round earth's shore
Lay like the folds of a bright girdle furled.
But now I only hear
Its melancholy, long, withdrawing roar,
Retreating, to the breath
Of the night-wind, down the vast edges drear
And naked shingles of the world.

Ah, love, let us be true
To one another! for the world, which seems
To lie before us like a land of dreams,
So various, so beautiful, so new,
Hath really neither joy, nor love, nor light,
Nor certitude, nor peace, nor help for pain;
And we are here as on a darkling plain
Swept with confused alarms of struggle and flight,
Where ignorant armies clash by night.

EMILY BRONTË

[1818–1848]

Stanzas

Often rebuked, yet always back returning
  To those first feelings that were born with me,
And leaving busy chase of wealth and learning
  For idle dreams of things that cannot be:

To-day, I will seek not the shadowy region;
  Its unsustaining vastness waxes drear;
And visions rising, legion after legion,
  Bring the unreal world too strangely near.

I'll walk, but not in old heroic traces,
  And not in paths of high morality,
And not among the half-distinguished faces,
  The clouded forms of long-past history.

I'll walk where my own nature would be leading:
  It vexes me to choose another guide:
Where the gray flocks in ferny glens are feeding;
  Where the wild wind blows on the mountain side.

What have those lonely mountains worth revealing?
  More glory and more grief than I can tell:
The earth that wakes *one* human heart to feeling
  Can centre both the worlds of Heaven and Hell.

WILLIAM CULLEN BRYANT
[1794–1878]

To a Waterfowl

Whither, 'midst falling dew,
While glow the heavens with the last steps of day,
Far, through their rosy depths, dost thou pursue
   Thy solitary way?

   Vainly the fowler's eye
Might mark thy distant flight to do thee wrong,
As, darkly painted on the crimson sky,
   Thy figure floats along.

   Seek'st thou the plashy brink
Of weedy lake, or marge of river wide,
Or where the rocking billows rise and sink
   On the chafed ocean side?

   There is a Power whose care
Teaches thy way along that pathless coast,—
The desert and illimitable air,—
   Lone wandering, but not lost.

All day thy wings have fanned,
At that far height, the cold, thin atmosphere,
Yet stoop not, weary, to the welcome land,
  Though the dark night is near.

And soon that toil shall end;
Soon shalt thou find a summer home, and rest,
And scream among thy fellows; reeds shall bend,
  Soon, o'er thy sheltered nest.

Thou'rt gone, the abyss of heaven
Hath swallowed up thy form; yet, on my heart
Deeply hath sunk the lesson thou hast given,
  And shall not soon depart.

He who, from zone to zone,
Guides through the boundless sky thy certain flight,
In the long way that I must tread alone,
  Will lead my steps aright.

GEORGE G. N., LORD BYRON
[1788–1824]

FROM *Childe Harold's Pilgrimage*

Canto IV, 1–3

I stood in Venice, on the Bridge of Sighs,
A palace and a prison on each hand:
I saw from out the wave her structures rise
As from the stroke of the enchanter's wand:
A thousand years their cloudy wings expand
Around me, and a dying Glory smiles
O'er the far times, when many a subject land
Looked to the wingéd Lion's marble piles,
Where Venice sate in state, throned on her hundred isles!

She looks a sea Cybele, fresh from ocean,
Rising with her tiara of proud towers
At airy distance, with majestic motion,
A ruler of the waters and their powers:
And such she was—her daughters had their dowers
From spoils of nations, and the exhaustless East

Poured in her lap all gems in sparkling showers:
In purple was she robed, and of her feast
Monarchs partook, and deemed their dignity increased.

In Venice Tasso's echoes are no more,
And silent rows the songless gondolier;
Her palaces are crumbling to the shore,
And music meets not always now the ear:
Those days are gone—but Beauty still is here;
States fall, arts fade—but Nature doth not die,
Nor yet forget how Venice once was dear,
The pleasant place of all festivity,
The revel of the earth, the masque of Italy!

EMILY DICKINSON
[1830–1886]

A narrow Fellow in the Grass

A narrow Fellow in the Grass
Occasionally rides—
You may have met Him—did you not
His notice sudden is—

The Grass divides as with a Comb—
A spotted shaft is seen—
And then it closes at your feet
And opens further on—

He likes a Boggy Acre
A floor too cool for Corn—
Yet when a Boy, and Barefoot—
I more than once at Noon
Have passed, I thought, a Whip lash
Unbraiding in the Sun
When stooping to secure it
It wrinkled, and was gone—

Several of Nature's People
I know, and they know me—
I feel for them a transport
Of cordiality—

But never met this Fellow
Attended, or alone
Without a tighter breathing
And Zero at the Bone—

EMILY DICKINSON

[1830–1886]

Because I could not stop for Death

Because I could not stop for Death—
He kindly stopped for me—
The Carriage held but just Ourselves—
And Immortality.

We slowly drove—He knew no haste
And I had put away
My labor and my leisure too,
For his Civility—

We passed the School, where Children strove
At Recess—in the Ring—
We passed the Fields of Gazing Grain—
We passed the Setting Sun—

Or rather—He passed Us—
The Dews drew quivering and chill—
For only Gossamer, my Gown—
My Tippet—only Tulle—

We paused before a House that seemed
A Swelling of the Ground—
The Roof was scarcely visible—
The Cornice—in the Ground—

Since then—'tis Centuries—and yet
Feels shorter than the Day
I first surmised the Horses' Heads
Were toward Eternity—

ROBERT FROST

[1874–1963]

Mending Wall

Something there is that doesn't love a wall,
That sends the frozen-ground-swell under it,
And spills the upper boulders in the sun;
And makes gaps even two can pass abreast.
The work of hunters is another thing:
I have come after them and made repair
Where they have left not one stone on a stone,
But they would have the rabbit out of hiding,
To please the yelping dogs. The gaps I mean,
No one has seen them made or heard them made,
But at spring mending-time we find them there.
I let my neighbor know beyond the hill;
And on a day we meet to walk the line
And set the wall between us once again.
We keep the wall between us as we go.
To each the boulders that have fallen to each.
And some are loaves and some so nearly balls
We have to use a spell to make them balance:
"Stay where you are until our backs are turned!"
We wear our fingers rough with handling them.

Oh, just another kind of outdoor game,
One on a side. It comes to little more:
There where it is we do not need the wall:
He is all pine and I am apple orchard.
My apple trees will never get across
And eat the cones under his pines, I tell him.
He only says, "Good fences make good neighbors."
Spring is the mischief in me, and I wonder
If I could put a notion in his head:
"*Why* do they make good neighbors? Isn't it
Where there are cows? But here there are no cows.
Before I built a wall I'd ask to know
What I was walling in or walling out,
And to whom I was like to give offense.
Something there is that doesn't love a wall,
That wants it down." I could say "Elves" to him,
But it's not elves exactly, and I'd rather
He said it for himself. I see him there
Bringing a stone grasped firmly by the top
In each hand, like an old-stone savage armed.
He moves in darkness as it seems to me,
Not of woods only and the shade of trees.
He will not go behind his father's saying,
And he likes having thought of it so well
He says again, "Good fences make good neighbors."

ROBERT FROST

[1874–1963]

Hyla Brook

By June our brook's run out of song and speed.
Sought for much after that, it will be found
Either to have gone groping underground
(And taken with it all the Hyla breed
That shouted in the mist a month ago,
Like ghost of sleigh bells in a ghost of snow)—
Or flourished and come up in jewelweed,
Weak foliage that is blown upon and bent
Even against the way its waters went.
Its bed is left a faded paper sheet
Of dead leaves stuck together by the heat—
A brook to none but who remember long.
This as it will be seen is other far
Than with brooks taken otherwhere in song.
We love the things we love for what they are.

ROBERT FROST

[1874–1963]

Spring Pools

These pools that, though in forests, still reflect
The total sky almost without defect,
And like the flowers beside them, chill and shiver,
Will the flowers beside them soon be gone,
And yet not out by any brook or river,
But up by roots to bring dark foliage on.
The trees that have it in their pent-up buds
To darken nature and be summer woods—
Let them think twice before they use their powers
To blot out and drink up and sweep away
These flowery waters and these watery flowers
From snow that melted only yesterday.

THOMAS HARDY

[1840–1928]

The Darkling Thrush

I leant upon a coppice gate
　When Frost was spectre-gray,
And Winter's dregs made desolate
　The weakening eye of day.
The tangled bine-stems scored the sky
　Like strings of broken lyres,
And all mankind that haunted nigh
　Had sought their household fires.

The land's sharp features seemed to be
　The Century's corpse outleant,
His crypt the cloudy canopy,
　The wind his death-lament.
The ancient pulse of germ and birth
　Was shrunken hard and dry,
And every spirit upon earth
　Seemed fervourless as I.

At once a voice arose among
　The bleak twigs overhead

In a full-hearted evensong
　　Of joy illimited;
An aged thrush, frail, gaunt, and small,
　　In blast-beruffled plume,
Had chosen thus to fling his soul
　　Upon the growing gloom.

So little cause for carolings
　　Of such ecstatic sound
Was written on terrestrial things
　　Afar or nigh around,
That I could think there trembled through
　　His happy good-night air
Some blessed Hope, whereof he knew
　　And I was unaware.

OLIVER WENDELL HOLMES

[1809–1894]

The Chambered Nautilus

This is the ship of pearl, which, poets feign,
    Sails the unshadowed main,
    The venturous bark that flings
On the sweet summer wind its purpled wings
In gulfs enchanted, where the Siren sings,
    And coral reefs lie bare,
Where the cold sea-maids rise to sun their streaming hair.

Its webs of living gauze no more unfurl;
    Wrecked is the ship of pearl!
    And every chambered cell,
Where its dim dreaming life was wont to dwell,
As the frail tenant shaped his growing shell,
    Before thee lies revealed,
Its irised ceiling rent, its sunless crypt unsealed!

Year after year beheld the silent toil
    That spread his lustrous coil;
    Still, as the spiral grew,
He left the past year's dwelling for the new,

Stole with soft step its shining archway through,
    Built up its idle door,
Stretched in his last-found home, and knew the old no more.

Thanks for the heavenly message brought by thee,
    Child of the wandering sea,
    Cast from her lap, forlorn!
From thy dead lips a clearer note is born
Than ever Triton blew from wreathéd horn!
    While on mine ear it rings,
Through the deep caves of thought I hear a voice that sings:

Build thee more stately mansions, O my soul,
    As the swift seasons roll!
    Leave thy low-vaulted past!
Let each new temple, nobler than the last,
Shut thee from heaven with a dome more vast,
    Till thou at length art free,
Leaving thine outgrown shell by life's unresting sea!

Spring and Fall

To a Young Child

Margaret, are you grieving
Over Goldengrove unleaving?
Leaves, like the things of man, you
With your fresh thoughts care for, can you?
Ah! as the heart grows older
It will come to such sights colder
By and by, nor spare a sigh
Though worlds of wanwood leafmeal lie;
And yet you *will* weep and know why.
Now no matter, child, the name:
Sorrow's springs are the same.
Nor mouth had, no nor mind, expressed
What heart heard of, ghost guessed:
It is the blight man was born for,
It is Margaret you mourn for.

JOHN KEATS

[1795–1821]

To Autumn

1

Season of mists and mellow fruitfulness,
   Close bosom-friend of the maturing sun;
Conspiring with him how to load and bless
   With fruit the vines that round the thatch-eaves run;
To bend with apples the mossed cottage-trees,
   And fill all fruit with ripeness to the core;
      To swell the gourd, and plump the hazel shells
   With a sweet kernel; to set budding more,
And still more, later flowers for the bees,
   Until they think warm days will never cease,
      For Summer has o'er-brimmed their clammy cells.

2

Who hath not seen thee oft amid thy store?
   Sometimes whoever seeks abroad may find
Thee sitting careless on a granary floor,
   Thy hair soft-lifted by the winnowing wind;
Or on a half-reaped furrow sound asleep,
   Drowsed with the fume of poppies, while thy hook

Spares the next swath and all its twinéd flowers:
And sometimes like a gleaner thou dost keep
   Steady thy laden head across a brook;
   Or by a cider-press, with patient look,
      Thou watchest the last oozings hours by hours.

3

Where are the songs of Spring? Aye, where are they?
   Think not of them, thou hast thy music too—
While barréd clouds bloom the soft-dying day,
   And touch the stubble-plains with rosy hue;
Then in a wailful choir the small gnats mourn
   Among the river sallows, borne aloft
   Or sinking as the light wind lives or dies;
And full-grown lambs loud bleat from hilly bourn;
   Hedge crickets sing; and now with treble soft
   The redbreast whistles from a garden-croft;
      And gathering swallows twitter in the skies.

WALTER SAVAGE LANDOR
[1775–1864]

On His Seventy-fifth Birthday

I strove with none; for none was worth my strife,
　Nature I loved, and next to Nature, Art;
I warmed both hands before the fire of life,
　It sinks, and I am ready to depart.

HENRY WADSWORTH LONGFELLOW

[1807–1882]

Snow-Flakes

Out of the bosom of the Air,
   Out of the cloud-folds of her garments shaken,
Over the woodlands brown and bare,
   Over the harvest-fields forsaken,
      Silent, and soft, and slow
      Descends the snow.

Even as our cloudy fancies take
   Suddenly shape in some divine expression,
Even as the troubled heart doth make
   In the white countenance confession,
      The troubled sky reveals
      The grief it feels.

This is the poem of the air,
   Slowly in silent syllables recorded;
This is the secret of despair,
   Long in its cloudy bosom hoarded,
      Now whispered and revealed
      To wood and field.

HENRY WADSWORTH LONGFELLOW
[1807–1882]

The Tide Rises, the Tide Falls

The tide rises, the tide falls,
The twilight darkens, the curlew calls;
Along the sea-sands damp and brown
The traveller hastens toward the town,
   And the tide rises, the tide falls.

Darkness settles on roofs and walls,
But the sea, the sea in the darkness calls;
The little waves, with their soft, white hands,
Efface the footprints in the sands,
   And the tide rises, the tide falls.

The morning breaks; the steeds in their stalls
Stamp and neigh, as the hostler calls;
The day returns, but nevermore
Returns the traveller to the shore,
   And the tide rises, the tide falls.

HERMAN MELVILLE

[1819–1891]

Shiloh

A Requiem (April, 1862)

Skimming lightly, wheeling still,
  The swallows fly low
Over the field in clouded days,
  The forest-field of Shiloh—
Over the field where April rain
Solaced the parched ones stretched in pain
Through the pause of night
That followed the Sunday fight
  Around the church of Shiloh—
The church so lone, the log-built one,
That echoed to many a parting groan
    And natural prayer
  Of dying foemen mingled there—
Foemen at morn, but friends at eve—
  Fame or country least their care:
(What like a bullet can undeceive!)
  But now they lie low,
While over them the swallows skim,
  And all is hushed at Shiloh.

EDWIN MUIR
[1887–1959]

The Animals

They do not live in the world,
Are not in time and space,
From birth to death hurled
No word do they have, not one
To plant a foot upon,
Were never in any place.

For by words the world was called
Out of the empty air,
With words was shaped and walled—
Line and circle and square,
Mud and emerald,—
Snatched from deceiving death
By the articulate breath.

But these have never trod
Twice the familiar track,
Never never turned back
Into the memoried day;
All is new and near

In the unchanging Here
Of the fifth great day of God,
That shall remain the same,
Never shall pass away.

On the sixth day we came.

EDWIN ARLINGTON ROBINSON

[1869–1935]

The House on the Hill

They are all gone away,
  The House is shut and still,
There is nothing more to say.

Through broken walls and gray
  The winds blow bleak and shrill:
They are all gone away.

Nor is there one to-day
  To speak them good or ill:
There is nothing more to say.

Why is it then we stray
  Around the sunken sill?
They are all gone away,

And our poor fancy-play
  For them is wasted skill:
There is nothing more to say.

There is ruin and decay
   In the House on the Hill:
They are all gone away,
There is nothing more to say.

PERCY BYSSHE SHELLEY

[1792–1822]

FROM *Adonais*

49–52

49

Go thou to Rome,—at once the Paradise,
   The grave, the city, and the wilderness;
   And where its wrecks like shattered mountains rise,
   And flowering weeds, and fragrant copses dress
   The bones of Desolation's nakedness
   Pass, till the spirit of the spot shall lead
   Thy footsteps to a slope of green access
   Where, like an infant's smile, over the dead
A light of laughing flowers along the grass is spread;

50

And gray walls moulder round, on which dull Time
   Feeds, like slow fire upon a hoary brand;
   And one keen pyramid with wedge sublime,
   Pavilioning the dust of him who planned
   This refuge for his memory, doth stand
   Like flame transformed to marble; and beneath,

A field is spread, on which a newer band
Have pitched in Heaven's smile their camp of death,
Welcoming him we lose with scarce extinguished breath.

51

Here pause: these graves are all too young as yet
To have outgrown the sorrow which consigned
Its charge to each; and if the seal is set,
Here, on one fountain of a mourning mind,
Break it not thou! too surely shalt thou find
Thine own well full, if thou returnest home,
Of tears and gall. From the world's bitter wind
Seek shelter in the shadow of the tomb.
What Adonais is, why fear we to become?

52

The One remains, the many change and pass;
Heaven's light forever shines, Earth's shadows fly;
Life, like a dome of many-coloured glass,
Stains the white radiance of Eternity,
Until Death tramples it to fragments.—Die,
If thou wouldst be with that which thou dost seek!
Follow where all is fled!—Rome's azure sky,
Flowers, ruins, statues, music, words, are weak
The glory they transfuse with fitting truth to speak.

STEVIE SMITH

[1902–1971]

Not Waving but Drowning

Nobody heard him, the dead man,
But still he lay moaning:
I was much further out than you thought
And not waving but drowning.

Poor chap, he always loved larking
And now he's dead
It must have been too cold for him his heart gave way,
They said.

Oh, no no no, it was too cold always
(Still the dead one lay moaning)
I was much too far out all my life
And not waving but drowning.

TRUMBULL STICKNEY

[1874–1904]

Mnemosyne

It's autumn in the country I remember

How warm a wind blew here about the ways!
And shadows on the hillside lay to slumber
During the long sun-sweetened summer-days.

It's cold abroad the country I remember.

The swallows veering skimmed the golden grain
At midday with a wing aslant and limber;
And yellow cattle browsed upon the plain

It's empty down the country I remember.

I had a sister lovely in my sight:
Her hair was dark, her eyes were very sombre;
We sang together in the woods at night.

It's lonely in the country I remember.

The babble of our children fills my ears,
And on our hearth I stare the perished ember
To flames that show all starry thro' my tears.

It's dark about the country I remember.

There are the mountains where I lived. The path
Is slushed with cattle-tracks and fallen timber,
The stumps are twisted by the tempests' wrath.

But that I knew these places are my own,
I'd ask how came such wretchedness to cumber
The earth, and I to people it alone.

It rains across the country I remember.

ALFRED, LORD TENNYSON
[1809–1892]

Ulysses

It little profits that an idle king,
By this still hearth, among these barren crags,
Matched with an aged wife, I mete and dole
Unequal laws unto a savage race,
That hoard, and sleep, and feed, and know not me.
I cannot rest from travel; I will drink
Life to the lees. All times I have enjoyed
Greatly, have suffered greatly, both with those
That loved me, and alone; on shore, and when
Through scudding drifts the rainy Hyades
Vext the dim sea. I am become a name;
For always roaming with a hungry heart
Much have I seen and known—cities of men
And manners, climates, councils, governments,
Myself not least, but honored of them all,—
And drunk delight of battle with my peers,
Far on the ringing plains of windy Troy.
I am a part of all that I have met;
Yet all experience is an arch wherethrough
Gleams that untraveled world whose margin fades

For ever and for ever when I move.
How dull it is to pause, to make an end,
To rust unburnished, not to shine in use!
As though to breathe were life! Life piled on life
Were all too little, and of one to me
Little remains; but every hour is saved
From that eternal silence, something more,
A bringer of new things; and vile it were
For some three suns to store and hoard myself,
And this gray spirit yearning in desire
To follow knowledge like a sinking star,
Beyond the utmost bound of human thought.

 This is my son, mine own Telemachus,
To whom I leave the scepter and the isle,
Well-loved of me, discerning to fulfill
This labor, by slow prudence to make mild
A rugged people, and through soft degrees
Subdue them to the useful and the good.
Most blameless is he, centered in the sphere
Of common duties, decent not to fail
In offices of tenderness, and pay
Meet adoration to my household gods,
When I am gone. He works his work, I mine.

 There lies the port; the vessel puffs her sail;
There gloom the dark, broad seas. My mariners,
Souls that have toiled, and wrought, and thought with me,
That ever with a frolic welcome took
The thunder and the sunshine, and opposed
Free hearts, free foreheads—you and I are old;
Old age hath yet his honor and his toil.
Death closes all; but something ere the end,
Some work of noble note, may yet be done,
Not unbecoming men that strove with gods.

The lights begin to twinkle from the rocks;
The long day wanes; the slow moon climbs; the deep
Moans round with many voices. Come, my friends,
'Tis not too late to seek a newer world.
Push off, and sitting well in order smite
The sounding furrows; for my purpose holds
To sail beyond the sunset, and the baths
Of all the western stars, until I die.
It may be that the gulfs will wash us down;
It may be we shall touch the Happy Isles,
And see the great Achilles, whom we knew.
Though much is taken, much abides; and though
We are not now that strength which in old days
Moved earth and heaven, that which we are, we are,
One equal temper of heroic hearts,
Made weak by time and fate, but strong in will
To strive, to seek, to find, and not to yield.

ALFRED, LORD TENNYSON
[1809–1892]

FROM *In Memoriam*

4

To Sleep I give my powers away;
My will is bondsman to the dark;
I sit within a helmless bark,
And with my heart I muse and say:

O heart, how fares it with thee now,
That thou should fail from thy desire,
Who scarcely darest to inquire,
"What is it makes me beat so low?"

Something it is which thou hast lost,
Some pleasure from thine early years.
Break thou deep vase of chilling tears,
That grief hath shaken into frost!

Such clouds of nameless trouble cross
   All night below the darkened eyes;
   With morning wakes the will, and cries,
"Thou shalt not be the fool of loss."

ALFRED, LORD TENNYSON

[1809–1892]

The Kraken

Below the thunders of the upper deep,
Far, far beneath in the abysmal sea,
His ancient, dreamless, uninvaded sleep
The Kraken sleepeth: faintest sunlights flee
About his shadowy sides; above him swell
Huge sponges of millennial growth and height;
And far away into the sickly light,
From many a wondrous grot and secret cell
Unnumbered and enormous polypi
Winnow with giant arms the slumbering green.
There hath he lain for ages, and will lie
Battening upon huge sea worms in his sleep,
Until the latter fire shall heat the deep;
Then once by man and angels to be seen,
In roaring he shall rise and on the surface die.

WALT WHITMAN
[1819–1892]

A noiseless patient spider

A noiseless patient spider,
I mark'd where on a little promontory it stood isolated,
Mark'd how to explore the vacant vast surrounding,
It launch'd forth filament, filament, filament, out of itself,
Ever unreeling them, ever tirelessly speeding them.

And you O my soul where you stand,
Surrounded, detached, in measureless oceans of space,
Ceaselessly musing, venturing, throwing, seeking the spheres to connect
   them,
Till the bridge you will need be form'd, till the ductile anchor hold,
Till the gossamer thread you fling catch somewhere, O my soul.

ACKNOWLEDGMENTS

We would like to thank all the authors, publishers, and literary representatives who have given permission to reprint poems in this collection. Every effort has been made to trace copyright holders. We will be glad to make good any errors or omissions in future editions.

ELIZABETH BISHOP: to Farrar, Straus and Giroux, Inc. for "Sonnet," from *The Complete Poems 1927–1979* by Elizabeth Bishop. Copyright © 1979, 1983 by Alice Helen Methfessel.

WILLIAM CARLOS WILLIAMS: to New Directions Publishing Corporation for "The Widow's Lament in Springtime," from *Collected Poems: 1909–1939, Volume I.* Copyright © 1938.

DYLAN THOMAS: to New Directions Publishing Corporation for "Do not go gentle into that good night," from *The Poems of Dylan Thomas*. Copyright © 1952 by Dylan Thomas.

STEVIE SMITH: to New Directions Publishing Corporation for "Not Waving but Drowning," from *Collected Poems of Stevie Smith*. Copyright © 1972 by Stevie Smith.

JOHN CROWE RANSOM: to Alfred A. Knopf for "Piazza Piece," from *Selected Poems*. Copyright © 1927 Alfred A. Knopf, Inc.; © renewed 1955 by John Crowe Ransom.

W. H. AUDEN: "Lay your sleeping head, my love," from *Collected Shorter Poems 1927–1957*. Copyright 1940 and renewed 1968 by W. H. Auden. Reprinted by permission of Faber & Faber Ltd., and Random House.

John Hollander is A. Bartlett Giamatti Professor of English at Yale University and has served as a Chancellor of The Academy of American Poets since 1981. His first book of poetry, *A Crackling of Thorns*, was selected by W. H. Auden as the 1958 volume in the Yale Series of Younger Poets. He has since published fifteen collections of poetry, most recently *Selected Poetry* and *Tesserae and Other Poems*. Mr. Hollander is also the author of several volumes of criticism and the editor of a number of anthologies, including the two-volume *American Poetry: The Nineteenth Century*.

Members of the advisory committee for *Committed to Memory* include Eavan Boland, Thom Gunn, Rachel Hadas, Michael Harper, Anthony Hecht, Maxine Kumin, J. D. McClatchy, Robert Pinsky, Mona Van Duyn, Rosanna Warren, and Richard Wilbur.